HOW TO MAKE EXHIBITIONS WORK
FOR YOUR BUSINESS

The Daily Telegraph
A BUSINESS ENTERPRISE BOOK

How to
MAKE
EXHIBITIONS
WORK FOR YOUR
BUSINESS

JOHN TALBOT

**KOGAN
PAGE**

Acknowledgements

Thanks are due to Reed Exhibition Companies Limited, Manchester Exhibition and Events Centre, National Exhibition Centre, Earls Court and Olympia and the Scottish Exhibition and Conference Centre for kind permission to reproduce their copyright illustrations.

First published in Great Britain in 1989 by Kogan Page Limited, 120 Pentonville Road, London N1 9JN.

British Library Cataloguing in Publication Data
Talbot, John
    How to make exhibitions work for your business.
    1. Trade exhibitions. Organisations
    I. Title
    659.1′52

ISBN 1-85091-995-X
ISBN 1-85091-996-8 Pbk

Printed and bound in Great Britain by Biddles Limited, Guildford

Contents

Foreword

Derek K Lyons, OBE
Chief Executive, Scottish Exhibition and Conference Centre

I am pleased to have been invited to write a foreword to this publication, particularly because I believe that its issue is timely.

The last few years have seen a burgeoning in the UK exhibition industry. Indeed, it seems that as fast as venues create extra space, exhibitions arise to fill it, and the UK probably has a greater diversity of exhibitions covering a broader spectrum and serving a wider variety of industries than any other country in Europe.

This growth is, I believe, a direct reflection of an increasing awareness on the part of UK companies of the essential place of exhibitions in their total marketing mix. And yet, despite the exceptional growth, we still lag well behind our European competitors, particularly those in Germany whose exhibitions do 'bestride the world like a Colossus'. It is reliably estimated that 24 per cent of all advertising and promotion expenditure in Germany is devoted to exhibitions compared with some 8 per cent in the UK.

The advent of the single European market in 1992 should alert us to the need to promote ourselves much more aggressively and to appreciate to a much greater extent the role which exhibitions have to play in that promotion.

One suspects that the small to medium companies intuitively feel that exhibitions are 'difficult' and expensive but I believe they have not really assessed their cost-effectiveness when compared with other media.

This admirable publication is designed for just those companies. Easy to read, well arranged, detailed, objective and informative, it clears away the preconceived ideas and misconceptions and provides an admirable guide into the realm of exhibitions which is much less arcane than is popularly supposed!

It has the great virtue of having been written, not by a theoretician, but by a practitioner and I warmly commend it to all those who are seeking a new, unique and effective means of communication with their customers and, much more importantly, with customers of whom they are not even yet aware.

Index of advertisers

Introduction

The forerunner of all major international exhibitions was the Great Exhibition of 1851 held at Crystal Palace, then in London's Hyde Park, and opened by Queen Victoria and Prince Albert. This exhibition brought together for the first time the best of manufactured goods from all over the world. Over the four and a half months the exhibition ran, 6 million people visited the 18-acre site. Other international exhibitions in Europe followed.

Exhibitions both large and small, national and international, trade or consumer have continued to flourish and to grow with more and more British companies participating in them. Exhibitions have also become more specialised. Most industries now have their own regular UK trade show perhaps slotting into a larger international event or a smaller, more specialised national show.

The aim of this book is to introduce small businesses to the role of exhibitions in their overall marketing and sales strategy. The most important question to ask is whether or not to exhibit. Once this decision has been made and your target market identified, then plans ranging over the next 18 months or two years should be examined. Most importantly, these plans must include budgets. Another important consideration is the stand design, construction type and any special packages that can be obtained. When the exhibition is over how do you analyse its success? Evaluating performance and follow-up is a key aspect of any exhibition plan. Useful contact addresses are listed on page 111.

Exhibitions and trade fairs have a very important role to play in the marketing strategy of any business. By their very presence at a trade fair, exhibition visitors are interested in the products on display there, and in buying them. These types of event, therefore, are a key opportunity for potential buyers to meet potential sellers. Exhibitions allow a business to display comprehensively its goods and services direct to a captive audience.

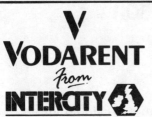

British companies in the 1960s and early 1970s undervalued the potential of exhibitions. As international trade became more competitive, UK companies started to re-evaluate the use of both national and international exhibitions. In 1976 the National Exhibition Centre was opened near Birmingham, and a long overdue purpose-built venue was created. Exhibition centres have now sprung up throughout the UK and attract over 9.5 million visitors annually. New venues opened in the 1980s include the Scottish Exhibition and Conference Centre in Glasgow, G-Mex in Manchester, Olympia 2 and the Arena in London. Many established venues have increased their capacity to meet the demand for more space, including the National Exhibition Centre which added a further 20,000 square metres of exhibition space in 1989. In 1988 the UK exhibition industry generated in excess of £1 billion. Companies now spend more on exhibitions than on advertising in magazines, periodicals or in national or technical journals. The use of exhibitions as a marketing tool can only increase as British industry learns to become more assertive and more aggressive in order to grow and survive in the increasingly competitive international market.

The part exhibitions can play in increasing their profitability is of key interest and importance to many small and medium-sized businesses. But there are pitfalls to be avoided, and the following chapters offer guidance and practical advice at every stage in the process for the benefit of both first-time and more experienced exhibitors.

Taking part in an exhibition can provide your business with enormous benefits, but it is also wise to remember and appreciate that an exhibition can involve virtually every aspect of marketing and promotion and, indeed, should if you intend to achieve the best results.

This book will give you practical advice and information to help you maximise the potential, but your own ideas and enthusiasm are still a major ingredient for a successful result. When organised professionally and with enthusiasm, your participation at an exhibition can be an enjoyable and rewarding experience. Like most things, if the preparation is completed with attention to detail and in good time, whether it's a meeting, a conference, product launch or an exhibition, you can be more relaxed to enjoy the fruits of your labour when the presentation or event takes place.

Top. *An aerial view of the National Exhibition Centre, Birmingham, showing the new halls and atrium in the foreground, linked to the central piazza by the skywalk.*

Bottom. *A trade show in progress in Hall 1 at the National Exhibition Centre.*

Top. *Hall 4 at the National Exhibition Centre showing catering facilities.*

Bottom. *Hall 4 with a consumer exhibition in progress.*

The Scottish Exhibition and Conference Centre has 19,000 square metres of net usable space with five interlinked halls grouped around the central concourse (seen here).

While you are likely to involve all aspects of the modern day marketing mix in your participation at an exhibition, the prime difference between the exhibition and all other marketing aids is that it takes business into the area of show business: you are on stage for all to see; as an exhibitor you are part of the cast, the industry creates the script, the exhibition organiser produces and directs, and the venue is the stage. When everyone pulls together, the exhibition is invariably successful and, as in show business, when you get it right the rewards can be tremendous.

1

So why exhibit?

In deciding whether or not to exhibit, the overriding question should be 'Can my company gain, as part of its corporate marketing strategy, a significant benefit from exhibiting?' This benefit may not be a monetary one. Indeed, you may have pinpointed two or more benefits together with subsidiary ones as well. For example, exhibiting could be part of your overall communications plan in order to build up better international outlets. By exhibiting you may be able to promote a new product or persuade the potential buyer that the quality or pricing structure on offer from your product is better than its competitors. Only you can decide on attending an exhibition because only you know what your company's marketing strategy is and how you see this role being fulfilled.

The decision to exhibit should not be taken solely because your competitors are taking a stand or have always taken a stand. Their needs and approach to attaining results could be totally different to your own. The cheapness of the stand rate is not a valid reason either. The organisers have a vested interest in selling you the space – the more stands sold the more representative of the industry the exhibition will be. On the other hand, if the event is not attracting interest from competitors, or if the organisers are offering space at reduced rates, then you need to ask the question, 'Why?' The best exhibitions are those that are fully supported by the industry they serve and comprehensively cover the product scope identified by the supporting trade associations or organiser.

Of all the marketing elements, exhibitions are unique in that they are an active, direct marketing platform bringing together both buyers and sellers and providing a unique opportunity of demonstrating your services or products. But exhibitions, whilst unique, incorporate other aspects of the marketing mix, and this is the reason that they should be part of your overall marketing plan. Whilst the aspects of public and press relations, advertisements, direct marketing and above and below the line promotion have a separate role to play, they also have an overlapping one where exhibitions are concerned. Your participation in an exhibition can successfully bring together all aspects of the marketing mix, focusing your company's product or service directly where and how you want it seen.

Even after you decide to exhibit, you should still ask the questions 'Why are we exhibiting? Do we still want to achieve from the exhibition what we started out with?' Always define clearly what your objectives are and reassess them. For example, which products or services do you want or need to show given the lead time? Which particular sales pitch do you wish to highlight? Will it change the overall product image (and most importantly, company image) that you want to project? Has the exhibition organiser targeted correctly the type of visitor most likely to be attracted to the exhibition and therefore, on to your stand? Lastly, is your marketing mix likely to change? And if so, why?

Before you decide which exhibition to go to, analyse your market. Which market segments are you trying to reach? What is the visitor attendance likely to be for the show, based on past shows? From this you should be able to ascertain the approximate number likely to be attracted to the forthcoming exhibition. Further, identify whether these visitors are likely to be professional, technical, or executive – in other words, are they the decision makers and are your products going to have a greater sales potential?

Which exhibition?

As exhibitions and trade shows are an increasingly essential part of the marketing mix in projecting your business, it is important to select the right show. The first question is, 'Should I be at a trade or a consumer event?' The answer is the former, if sales go through wholesalers and distributors, and the latter if direct selling methods are used. Rarely are the two used together. The second question to ask is 'Should

I exhibit at one show only or ought I to exhibit at a number of them?' You should study details of all exhibitions within your industrial sector which are taking place over an 18-month period. Your trade association will be able to supply a full list of forthcoming exhibitions. Information on most events can be obtained from *Exhibition Bulletin* which lists the many events held every year, not only in the UK but throughout the world. The Association of Exhibition Organisers (AEO) and the British Exhibition Contractors Association (BECA) should also be able to assist.

In determining which exhibition or exhibitions to attend, you need to evaluate your particular business needs. Do these needs dictate frequent exhibiting at specialised exhibitions, or would more general events be preferable?

Exhibitions sponsored by a specific industry trade association have grown in number and importance. If your firm is a member of an association, then discount terms might be available. However, discounts should not be a criterion when deciding whether or not to exhibit. Also ascertain the exhibition's past successes. How long has this trade fair been running? And if it is a new event, why is it being staged? These questions need to be answered before you include this exhibition in your plan.

Exhibitions are now being sponsored by both UK and overseas governments where importing or exporting opportunities may be available. The trade association that represents the industry or your local Chamber of Commerce might have had this responsibility delegated to them. If going overseas, certain participants could find themselves being sponsored by local or government money. Apart from overseas events, the Chambers of Commerce are also active when setting up local exhibitions. These events are staged either in the Chambers' offices or at local hotels. But again, before making any decisions, the same questions should be asked to evaluate whether or not this sort of venue would be beneficial to your overall plan (see Chapter 9).

There are also major international events organised in cycle with events in other countries. These are planned with considerable lead times (usually several years) and information about these events is available in *Exhibition Bulletin*. Naturally, this necessitates you planning well in advance also. As these events are usually well established, the previous

year's attendance should be known. Ask also whether or not
the organisers can give a breakdown of the attendance, listing status, size of company, job function and interest of the
visitor. This information will help you to judge the extent of
the likely response and the benefit obtainable from being at
that exhibition.

Armed with all this information, you can list in order of
priority which exhibitions or trade fairs it would be beneficial
to attend. What size are the facilities and where is the geographical location of these events? What are the stand costs?
Will they relate to your overall budget?

The cost of the floor space represents approximately 26
per cent of the cost of participating in an exhibition. Therefore, if you are taking a stand in three exhibitions, and the
floor space cost is £3,000 you should roughly allocate a total
of £12,000 to cover stand design and construction on site,
staffing, advertising and other indirect costs. If this is likely to
be out of bounds for your budget, then you have to rethink
your strategy. Chapter 2 discusses budgeting in detail.

If selecting two or more exhibitions to attend each year, try to ensure that these are spaced at reasonable intervals. Many small business are unable to meet a demanding and time-consuming exhibition schedule. The location of these exhibitions also needs careful thought as supplementary costs such as overnight accommodation, travel and so on need to be taken into account.

Analysing your needs

To be a successful exhibitor, you need to identify and set your objectives by analysing your needs. Once these are set, then the planning can be set in motion. Ask yourself why you are exhibiting, and what you want to achieve from it. Before identifying your exhibition objectives, you must first analyse your market. Which market segment are you trying to reach? Which prospective customers are likely to be at the show? What is the visitor breakdown and are these audited figures? Which products or features need to be shown, and are there any special features which need to be highlighted? What is the overall image that you wish to project?

The second stage in analysing your needs is to define what will actually be included in your exhibition. If you major on product display, will that help your sales? Will you be providing technical information on the stand or will you be concentrating on meeting and entertaining specific customers? Will demonstration equipment on the stand help sales? Are there any new features within your product range to be exploited? Will you be exhibiting your entire product range or just a few selected items? What is your overall sales target?

All these needs can be assessed together so that specific objectives can be quantified into achievable goals. The end results are the only meaningful way of assessing whether or not the event has been a successful one. Listed below are typical exhibition objectives. You might find it useful to prioritise your needs as they appear in this list or add any others.

- Meet existing customers
- Make new contacts
- Maintain and improve company image
- Maintain market share

- Enhance UK market share
- Enhance European/worldwide market share
- Prevent corroding of your market position
- Launch new product
- Find agents/distributors in UK/overseas
- Obtain competitive intelligence
- Take orders, open new accounts, process enquiries
- Re-establish current products
- Stimulate media coverage
- Entertain existing and new customers
- Distribute sales and promotional literature
- Stimulate corporate awareness
- Meet and observe competitors
- Conduct business with other exhibitors
- Acquire new customer data for direct mail.

Visitor profile

Most established exhibitions will have audited visitor figures, broken down into various categories. As each visitor arrives at an exhibition, they are given a registration card to fill out if they have not received one in advance as part of the admission ticket. The card ascertains the nature of the person's trade or business, the size of company, its location, the position the person holds in that company or organisation (whether or not he or she is the decision maker) and his or her general and particular interests. A breakdown of this information is found on the exhibition data form. After the previous exhibition has taken place, ask the organiser for the exhibition data form.

It is important for you to have these details to get an idea of the likely interest in your product. What you need to ascertain from the figures is the level of decision makers who attend the exhibition. It is these decision makers who need to be cultivated as this is where the future sales are generated. Thus in coming to the decision to exhibit at a particular exhibition, these audited figures are of prime importance.

Exhibitions v other marketing media

It is not within the scope of this book to state categorically that one marketing tool brings in more positive response than another. The success of a direct sales advertisement cannot be pitted against the number of sales prospects generated from having an exhibition stand at a trade fair. All aspects of your marketing strategy are collective and are for different purposes and produce different results – although there will be a certain overlap and you might find that if your objectives call for greater sales leads then, for example, direct marketing might produce the best results for your company. If you have used exhibitions before, you will have a good idea of where to place them on your media priority list. If you have not, your first experience should be comprehensively evaluated so you can determine the overall value of participation in relation to the marketing tools you are currently using. You know your needs better than anyone else and, therefore, only you can decide on the best methods to attain the desired results.

2

Budgeting for success

Realistic budget and controlling costs

How many times have you heard 'exhibiting is too expensive'? Participating in an exhibition can be costly but for most businesses it is an investment that shows positive returns and is now probably the most cost-effective way of generating sales. What is important, however, is to know, understand and control the various cost elements that make up your overall budget. This avoids unnecessary expense and improves the return on your exhibition investment.

When creating a realistic budget you need to divide costs into two areas. Firstly, there are the direct costs such as payment for the stand space, construction and fitting out of the stand, and other costs such as special literature. Secondly, there are indirect costs (sometimes known as hidden costs) such as staff time in preparing for the exhibition, expenses and other costs incurred whilst working on the exhibition and promoting it.

When preparing your budget it is worthwhile to segment your direct and indirect costs on your budget sheet. Remember to include all fixed costs from advertising your presence at the event in the national, local or trade press, to installing coffee-making facilities. A survey has been conducted by Industrial and Trade Fairs which revealed that the percentage of expenditure breaks down approximately as follows:

- Space rental – 26 per cent
- Stand services – 9 per cent (stand services include electrics, compressed air, water and waste, on-site handling and storage etc);

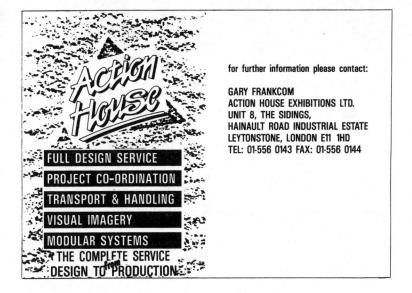

- Stand construction – 41 per cent (design, construction, graphics, furniture, etc);
- Staffing and facilities – 17 per cent (includes stand staffing, accommodation, transportation, entertaining, catering, etc);
- Publicity – 7 per cent (related promotions and publicity for the event).

Of this expenditure some 35 per cent of costs are determined by the exhibition organiser while the other 65 per cent are determined and controlled completely by you, the exhibitor.

Creating a budget

If you have not exhibited before then to ascertain the total cost of participating requires the creation of a realistic budget.

Consider the type of event that you will be exhibiting at. Look at the literature sent by the stand organiser, which will show the number of visitors, and more importantly, the type of visitor likely to attend. The point of the exhibition is to display your products/services and, therefore, to sell your products. Rather like a sales forecast, you should create an exhibition forecast of the number of sales prospects and sales closures that you expect over the duration of the exhibition and beyond. If you estimate you will close three or four sales at the show and possibly three to four further sales from leads generated by the show, work out what the value of these orders is likely to be. What is your profit margin on six to eight sales? Allocate between 25 per cent and 30 per cent of this value to your exhibition plus any additional amounts that you feel could be utilised as part of the expenditure, based upon the fact that an exhibition is promoting your company as well as your products and is therefore a marketing tool. This process can be used not just for one exhibition but for your company's annual or biannual exhibition programmes.

Let us assume that you have a working budget of £3,275. Of this your stand rental is £1,200 (i.e. a quarter of your costs). This includes the construction of your shell stand but the display items and furniture are extra at £400. A further £600 has been allocated for stand services; the installation of electrics, water and waste on site. As the organisers of the trade fair will be handling a great proportion of the publicity themselves you may decide not to spend money on leaflets etc, however, as an approximation, allow £275 for printing. The remainder of £300 is allocated to catering and entertaining on the stand, with a further £500 for accommodation and transport. These prices are based on a stand measuring 12 square metres, probably the smallest available at most exhibitions.

Controlling costs

Stand space rental is a direct or fixed cost. The amount that is charged is structured by the exhibition organiser and can range from £60 per square metre to over £200, depending on the exhibition. An average cost for 1989 would be £100 per square metre for a medium-sized national show. However, it is you who determine what you rent and how you use it. The rental cost charged by the organiser is determined by the stand size and, with some exhibitions, its location.

Your space rental costs are determined by the stand size you envisage you need. This is determined by your objectives which in turn are dictated by the size and number of products you wish to display, your demonstration requirements (both static and moving), the targeted number of stand visitors and staffing numbers, and whether or not you are to include a hospitality area on your stand. When deciding what your space requirements should be, care should be taken so that your budget is not overstretched. On the other hand, do not cut costs and try to put the maximum products per square foot/metre into stand space. This would only make your stand look cluttered and unappealing to passers-by.

Stand service costs

On-site services can be very expensive and you must carefully determine what you need and what you can afford. Good planning and awareness will help you control your stand services budget. Consider the following points carefully as these can quickly run up your stand services charge.

1 What will be our total requirement for electric power?
2 What are the start up and running loads for the machines?
3 Can some or all of our machines and lighting be run from a pre-wired and constructed control panel?
4 Will water and compressed air ratings enable us to make multiple connections?
5 Have our products been sited to gain the best advantage of the service inlets? (Most modern venues have under-floor ducted service inlets.)
6 What have we chosen to display:
   • photographs?
   • models?
   • static displays?
   • working displays?

It is important to remember that specific service requirements are channelled to your stand well in advance of your arrival. Should you have to order on the day the exhibition starts then this can incur extra cost, not to mention connection delays which cause distruption and inconvenience to your fellow exhibitors and to your stand visitors. Most exhibition sites are highly unionised, so do not think that you can just take out a screwdriver and adjust a sign or install electrics yourself. Exhibition organisers' rules have to be kept (see Chapter 8).

Planning is a main factor in controlling costs. To keep costs to a minimum you should:

- Select your product for display at an early stage;
- Ensure that your production programme has been finished and tested well in advance;
- Schedule the arrival of the products at a time convenient to yourselves, avoiding costly delays and disruption of stand-building schedule;
- Confirm once again your stand plan, locating where the products are to be placed.

If this is not done then costly unscheduled relifting and replacing of standing buildings will have to occur. Other areas for planning include:

- Adequate removal and storage space for packing cases (a cluttered stand site not only causes inconvenience and delays but can damage stand fittings and, worst of all, stand display equipment);
- A plan for repackaging, handling, lifting and transporting your exhibition after the event is over.

It is important to note what stand equipment can be used again for other exhibitions. This should be carefully packed away and any stand staff assisting should be made aware of the items.

If the exhibition is seen as the main launch pad for a new product or a new display of corporate imagery then the budget will have to take into account the extra money needed not only for stand design but promotions and entertainment. You must ascertain how much you can spend and what the event is worth to you. But bear in mind that the latest video and laser technology (if permitted by the organisers) is costly.

Watching out for indirect costs

Indirect costs can quickly run away with your budget money. It is worthwhile listing possible areas of expenditure.

1 Your time and the time of your staff in planning the event;

2   Expenses incurred for planning the event, visiting the site and the contractors;
3   Exhibition development costs;
4   Insurance;
5   Staffing of the exhibition stand;
6   Hotel accommodation during the exhibition;
7   Expenses incurred during the exhibition for entertainment (both staff and client);
8   Telephone calls made both to and from the stand;
9   Any special finishing touches required for your stand.

Certain fixed costs will be incurred whether or not your staff man the stand and whether or not they help prepare for the exhibition display of products. Whilst there is no hard and fast rule with regard to the proportion of indirect costs, it is prudent to follow a sensible budgeting policy. Past experience on costing these events will help, but for the newcomer a costing exercise on man-hours spent would prove valuable, is not difficult to do, and would also prove useful when budgeting for your next exhibition.

Cost-cutting areas

The stand space paid for is a direct or fixed cost and as such should not fluctuate. What you spend in fitments does. For example, how many tables and chairs do you need for your stand? Can these be reduced in any way without affecting your stand design? Have you elicited a number of quotes for the design and construction? Is it cheaper to have a hospitality area on your stand or to use the facilities provided by the exhibition? Are there two or more standards of floor covering varying in cost? Is a telephone essential? Have you costed out whether the shell scheme space (see page 32) is going to work out more cost effective than a special shell package scheme, provided by the organiser? It is likely that a shell package scheme will save you time and effort and be cheaper in the long term.

Be selective in what you choose to display on your stand but do bear in mind that you need to achieve your objectives. Drastically paring down on your budget can affect these. Photographs are the cheapest display material but unless the design is extremely well done, it will not be as effective as models, nor will models be as effective as the product on display, and a non-moving product on display in not as effective as a working exhibit. The more advanced and detailed the stand, the more it is going to cost. Realism when planning a stand is essential.

Certain exhibition organisers offer stand options where the exhibitor can select a basic shell or floor space with floor coverings an optional extra. For first-time or small exhibitors, this may be worthwhile provided you first ascertain what is included and how much the excluded but necessary elements will cost you. The organiser may also offer packages with 'all-in costs'. In other words, the organiser provides everything from the space itself to the stand design and fitments. Usually, this is less expensive but you have to cost out how much time you would have to spend organising the separate elements, what your time is worth and whether these figures equate to the price being quoted by the organisers.

How to book stand space

Stands at established trade exhibitions are likely to be booked many months in advance, sometimes more than 12 months before the event, so try not to leave booking your stand until the last few months before the exhibition takes place, as the choice of positions is likely to be limited.

Application forms for booking stand space are sent out with the organiser's sales literature, usually at least 12 months before the exhibition takes place. Read the fine print very carefully as it sets out all the contractual arrangements. Once these have been completed and returned the first instalment for the stand rental is due. There are usually three instalments with the final payment falling due a month before the exhibition starts.

There are usually two types of stand available Smaller businesses are unlikely to book large 60 square metre sites – instead they will be content with a 12 square metre site. For this capacity of space there is likely to be either a package stand or a shell stand. Only large rentals of floor space are likely to be of the space-only type. Whichever you book, make sure you know what is included and what is not. Should you at a later date decide you wish to move to another stand location then speak to the organisers as this is usually possible unless it is a last-minute decision.

Your contract will detail cancellation procedures which should be read very carefully. If you do have to cancel then the nearer the exhibition date, the more money you are likely to forfeit.

Failure to meet the deadlines indicated on the stand space contract could mean that you will not secure stand space. Naturally, the exhibition organisers need to ensure that all bookings are firm and that the potential exhibitor will not renege on the booking at the last moment, leaving a gap in the exhibition. Hence a first payment (usually 25 per cent) is required at an early stage and is usually non-returnable. There are strict rules with regard to cancellations, so before signing any exhibition booking form, the small print must be read carefully.

Basic stands for the smaller budget

Shell stand

The basic shell stand provided by exhibition organisers consists of a back wall and two dividing walls. It also comes with a fascia board on which your company's name is placed. Some organisers include floor covering – which can mean either floor tiles or carpet. No electrics or other amenities are provided (see Figure 2.1).

Shell package scheme

This scheme includes the shell together with electrics, floor covering, lights, and certain items of furniture. Display racks, shelving and in some cases a partitioned area for use as an office can also be provided (see Figure 2.2).

Modular system

For use throughout your exhibition programme, these stands are designed to be put up and taken down again, therefore they are made of durable materials.

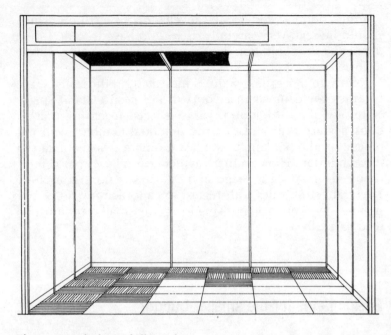

Figure 2.1 *The basic shell stand*
The basic shell stand consists of back wall, side panels and fascia board. It usually includes the signwriting of your company's name. It may include floor covering and a muslin ceiling. Always check the organiser's specification; sometimes floor covering is extra.

Purpose-built system

You hire your own designer and stand contractor to design and put up a stand which fits into the space allocated and conforms to the organiser's specifications.

Special purpose-built stand system

Some organisers have recently started to provide this type of stand. Although of modular construction, these stands provide a system of quality and individual design.

Each time an exhibition stand is used it is seen by the visitor as new. Whilst it is important to store stand equipment previously purchased, it must be redesigned for a fresh

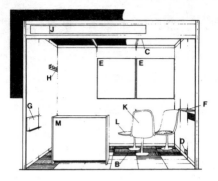

9 square metre stand. 3 metres wide x 3 metres deep.

The full specification for the stands: Back and side walls, together with the fascia board etc.

KEY	ITEM
B	Carpet Tiles. Choice of colours: Red, Blue, Yellow, Beige. Only one colour per stand.
C	1 x 8ft. fluorescent fitting fixed to the underside of the roof cross beams for maximum and even light spread.
D	1 x 13 amp square pin power socket 500 watt maximum load. Can only be fixed to aluminium uprights along back or side walls but at any height up to 2.43 metres.
E	2 x 980mm x 980mm softwood display panels felt covered to match carpet tiles and suspended by hanging straps 1m. from the floor to the underside of the panel.
F	1 display shelf 1.000m x 300mm white melamine finish. Fixed between aluminium wall uprights at 1.30m in drawing above.
G	1 x 4 compartment A4 literature rack with clear perspex front. Fixed between aluminium wall uprights at 900mm to the underside in drawing above.
H	1 hat and coat rack with 4 hooks. Suspended by metal hanging straps 1.70m from floor.
J	Stand number and Exhibitor's name panel. Company name only may appear here, no advertising slogans or logos will be accepted. Name in standard lettering, black on a white background with the stand number reversed white out of black.
K	2 - White Formed Side Chairs
L	1 - Circular White Coffee Table
M	1 - Lockable Storage Unit
N	1 - Wastepaper Bin
O	1 - Glass Ashtray

Figure 2.2 *A shell stand package scheme*
While this is a typical package scheme, they do vary; for instance, some organisers offer telephones. Check the cost of the package with what is being supplied.

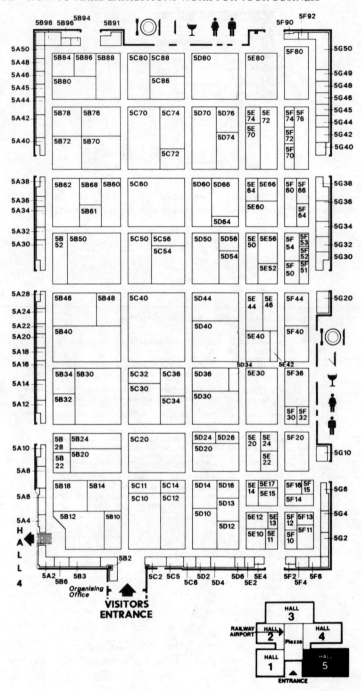

approach. If this is not done, you will not only have a dated exhibit but one that will not be as appealing as others in the hall, and your exhibition investment could be reduced.

One person should be appointed to have total authority for the organising and running of the event. This person should be responsible for direct costs, overseeing and accounting and should give authorisation for the indirect costs. In this way you can keep control of expenditure and be assured of a well-organised event.

When planning a stand, it is important to get the design and construction as you want it from the start. If you change your mind, then even small changes can cost money. This is why it is so important to brief the stand designer thoroughly, making sure he knows these needs.

Before accepting the design why not ask your workforce and your fellow managers' opinions? Apart from practising good management, this ensure that if any areas have been overlooked, fresh eyes cast over the design will pick up the omissions. If there is a consensus for any additions, then it could be worthwhile to include them. However, if there is no

---

Figure 2.3 *A typical floor plan*
Part of an international exhibition held at the National Exhibition Centre. The smaller stands around the perimeter are usually shell stands and most organisers designate perimeter stands shell only. The core of the hall is a mixture of shell stands and contractor purpose-designed stands; sizes vary from 12 square meters to many hundreds. This hall has two catering areas featuring waitress and self-service facilities, bars and toilets.

There are many contradictory arguments where best to site your stand. In a hall like this it's not *where* you site your stand that's so important, but rather *what you do* on the stand to attract customers. However, if one of your main priorities is to promote corporate image, a site opposite the main entrance would be useful. The organiser will show you a similar plan from which you will be asked to choose the location for your stand. If a specific site is offered to you and you feel it is too large the organiser will usually halve or quarter the site in question, so do not feel you have to take the whole site. On the other hand, you can combine two designated sites into one if you need the additional space; either way, the organiser is usually flexible.

sound marketing reason for changing the design, then it should be stuck to.

Lastly, if you are relying on others to supply the graphics, stand design and construction, ensure that the contractors know what their budget is. Be absolutely clear all along when briefing suppliers so that they know the amount of money allocated to them is for an all-inclusive supply. Likewise, if you have an assistant, make sure he or she knows what the budget constraints are. Getting the most out of an exhibition can depend on your arrival at a realistic monetary limit which will ensure you are not out of pocket, yet does nothing to hinder the potential success of the event.

3

The focal point

Stand design and construction

Winning customers, not design awards, should be the main criterion when planning your stand presentation. Elaborate, over-designed stands are now no longer the norm, the gin palace of the 1960s and 1970s having been replaced by more functional business-like presentation which is far more effective and saves money. The stand design that you choose should reflect the overall exhibition objectives. You should consider the business's desired image, the products being displayed, and the ability to be able to attract on to the stand the type of visitor/customer you have targeted. Overall, the exhibition stand is a place to house your exhibit and complement it, not overwhelm it. Think of the exhibition as an extension of your office/factory premises when planning your stand. A friendly atmosphere is conducive to selling.

If you are going for an individually designed stand and not a shell packaged scheme, you will be commissioning a stand designer (unless you have in-house expertise). For such a specialised function, unless you have been recommended to a good and experienced stand designer, then your next line of approach should be to contact the British Exhibition Contractors Association (BECA). The Association will be able to provide a list of their members so that you can select those nearest to you.

The next stage is to brief as early on as possible a stand designer. It cannot be stressed too often that the key to organising a successful exhibition is planning well in advance. Contact two or three designers and ask to see their work and who they have worked for. Shop around until you are satisfied that the person understands your brief, can meet the time scale and will design within the budget. But before appointing a designer, ask for references and do take these up with the clients to see that the work has been delivered on time and within the budget. It is important to see a number of his or her previous designs to make sure that they are attractive and eye catching. If an exhibition is currently on near you, and the designer has submitted designs for this, then it would be worthwhile visiting the exhibition to see how workable and how appealing the stand actually is.

Has the designer successfully produced designs for both static and free-moving equipment? Whether or not you eventually use this designer, it is useful for your own information to visit exhibitions to see what stand designs there are and what success they are having. New ideas are always appearing and viewing them might trigger off a more appropriate and appealing one to suit your needs.

While thoroughly briefing the stand designer, it is important to stress that you do require a flexibility of design so that you can select varying displays and adjust budget requirements accordingly. Do not feel shy about saying that the designs do not reflect your product's image and so on. Remember that the stand design accounts for approximately 9 per cent of your budget. So not only must you get value for money but more importantly the right visual impact must be achieved.

In briefing the designer, you should tell him what the firm's objectives are in having the stand, what products you want to display and whether or not they are static or moving, the correct name of the company or group of companies (avoid using trade names, the words 'company' and 'limited' can also be discarded), the budget constraints and the time scale. The designer must also know if you wish a hospitality section to be included on the stand and how many on-site personnel will be manning it.

The exhibition organiser will have supplied you with the dimensions of your stand, and these must be passed on to the designer. Further information of use to him or her will be the stand location, i.e. whether on a corner near to the exhibitions lounge or close to hospitality area. Information on the exact dimensions of the machines that will be on display and where they need to be placed is essential to the designer,

and should take the form of exact specifications for height,
weight, width and so on. Any errors made here can be a
nightmare should the equipment be too large for the stand.
Everything must be explained and re-explained if necessary
as once the design has been approved any alterations will be
expensive. Confirm every detail in writing.

Ask the exhibition organiser the most suitable entrance for
machinery, its height clearance and so on. This is important
as some exhibition centres have height constraints – for
example the Barbican has low ceilings in comparison with
the National Exhibition Centre. Find out what the organiser
includes in the price of the shell or package of the stand;
stand furniture or lights for example. Check the exhibition's
rules and regulations so that you are familiar with them and
also with any constraints that they might place on your stand
design. When you are briefing the designer, all this additional
information will need to be passed on. Any information is of
use, from whether or not water is needed for your display so
suitable drainage can be laid on, to extra voltage which is a
common requirement. Planning and controlling the cost of
your stand starts at this point. Overleaf is a brief checklist of
the points that need careful attention.

1   Familiarise yourself with the exhibition organiser's rules and regulations;
2   Obtain at least three competitive options and quotes from both designer and contractors. Take up references. See the work that they have done for other companies;
3   Fully brief the designer and confirm in writing the set parameters required by your stand to both the designers and to the contractors. Most importantly, note down the cost that has been agreed by all parties;
4   In writing, confirm your brief to the stand designer, incorporating your objectives for the exhibition;
5   When appointing a stand contractor ensure that they are reputable, reliable and competent and they are party to the national working rule agreement for the exhibition industry;
6   Set a time schedule for your stand both for design and building. Set a cost schedule and method of payment for both. Monitor the progress and expenditure at regular intervals;
7   Before making the final decision on design, ensure that everything has been allowed for and that nothing is missing from it. Changes at a later stage are not only time consuming but very expensive;
8   Make hotel reservations for the staff well in advance at a convenient location. Check transportation arrangements for both exhibits as well as personnel. This should be done at least 12 months in advance for major international events being held at the NEC or major London venues.

Useful design considerations

Stand design is an art. It takes the siting of the stand, links it with the client's objectives, allowing for any out-of-the-ordinary restrictions or design requirements and pulls together a display that is as welcoming as possible with all the interest and detail noted. It is not merely a question of knowing the stand dimensions and placing bookshelves in one corner and photographs across the back wall, it is the overall imagery and ambiance that the visual display projects. Certain exhibitions have themes and a good designer tries to incorporate this theme with your stand design.

Before finalising the design, there are a few design tips to bear in mind.

- Allow enough space for visitors to come on to the stand;
- Do not clutter a stand with products;
- Allow a focal point at the back of the stand to draw visitors in;
- Place brochures and leaflets in a strategic position so that enquiries have to be made to your staff.

If the stand design is unusual the organiser's rules state that they have to see and agree the plans. The rules and regulations laid down by the stand organiser must be kept to as breaking them in effect breaks your contract, see Chapter 7.

Briefing the stand contractor

The next stage is to brief a stand contractor. The designer may be able to recommend one to you. You can, of course, get in touch with the British Exhibition Contractors Association who will supply you with a list of members. Recommendations again should be sought and followed up.

Once a stand contractor has been decided upon, a thorough briefing is needed. Deadline dates should be confirmed and budget constraints agreed. Specific dates and times for collection and delivery of the stand and its equipment must be noted. A list of all items that have to be placed on the stand, including plant equipment, photographs or exhibition literature must be given to him. Confirm in writing.

The exhibition contractor's duty is to assemble and construct your exhibition stand according to the designer's brief. This is where the greatest proportion of your budget goes. Stand walls are usually constructed of a light, flat timber framework made of plywood. This wood, by law, has to be

treated with a fire retardant. More elaborate details, such as cornices, are shaped from chipboard. The floor is known as the platform. (A platform is essential for some venues as it carries the electrics and services but is not necessary for more modern venues, such as the NEC, where under-floor ducting is available.) Platforms are made of hardened chipboard supported with timbers placed at intervals. Painting and papering to cover all surfaces complete the job.

The more complicated the design, the more expensive the construction of the stand. For example, double decker stands have to satisfy local building inspectors because, as the name implies, they are literally one stand on top of another. Materials can get more exotic dependent upon the design. These can include silk screen panels with embossed logos or special designs.

Most of the construction systems used take the form of plated steel rods or tubes. Although not all materials used are standard sizes, the contractor has preconstructed materials so that the basic stand form can be made. If you envisage exhibiting half a dozen times a year and if your stand design is relatively simple, then it might be worthwhile buying a sturdy, hard-wearing and simple-to-erect system. Alternatively, the contractor might suggest that you select items in stock to make up your design so that these elements can be hired out to you for the duration of an exhibition. At the end the contractor can dismantle the stand, taking the hired items away.

The expense in designing and constructing the stand is in the labour. Putting the module together does not take very long but taking the module and all the extra parts to the location and then erecting the final display does take a considerable amount of time. Remember electrics, water and waste have to be connected, and at the end these have to be dismantled.

The stand is the responsibility of the exhibitor and not of the exhibition organiser. This means that if the stand has any out-of-the-ordinary elements attached to its structure, the governing authorities have to give approval. Any modification called for by these authorities will be expensive to implement but, obviously, will have to be done. For displays that incorporate moving machinery, the health and safety inspectors will need to be informed and the fire authorities informed of any displays that could turn out to be possible fire hazards. Building regulations cover the structure of any stand that does not conform to a basic design, for instance those with stairs, two floors or additional structures.

Display system *v* panel system

A display system incorporates display cases, any form of desk, cupboard and racking. As mentioned, you can buy sturdy, hard-wearing and easy-to-erect systems should you need more permanent display material. The more expensive display systems have a locking device. And security, at an exhibition, is something that must be considered.

A panel system is a large, usually concertina series of panels on which a motif, theme, company name or logo can be mounted. These panel systems are fairly robust being made out of hardened board and tubular steel and are relatively easy to erect being lightweight. They are useful in screening off part of the stand, where the tea and coffee-making facilities could be hidden for example. Panels can display photographs or posters. If purchasing one of these systems, do ensure that the framework is sturdy enough to stand handling.

Of the two the panel system is the easier to assemble. However, a combination of the two is common and allows for options in design and presentation.

A number of panel and display designs have been brought across from the US. These can be easily transported to trade fairs and dismantled quickly. There is a folding display system that can be assembled in a few minutes and when the exhibition is over, it can be folded down and fitted into a car boot. This system can be used for sales presentations as well as exhibition stands.

Making use of facilities

All exhibitions have some facilities on offer. These will range from hospitality facilities (including both food and beverage areas) to electrics and stand cleaning. When booking your stand space, it is important to find out from the organisers what is included in the price and what extra facilities are on offer and at what cost.

The organiser's officially approved contractor or the exhibition centre's contractor installs all the electrics, water and waste. Subject to the rules and regulations of the organisers, you are usually allowed to bring in your own contractor for specialised work but they must belong to the appropriate trade union. Stand cleaning usually means the cleaner for the exhibition vacuums the carpet and takes away the rubbish; it does not include washing up the coffee cups and glasses.

4

Making your presence felt – public relations and promotions

Each exhibitor on average will spend approximately 7 per cent of their total show budget on related promotions and publicity for use before, during and after the exhibition. The organisers of the exhibition will likewise spend a considerable portion of their budget on promoting the show to get the maximum number of visitors to attend. They will offer certain pre-publicity facilities such as the inclusion of your firm's name in leaflets and other promotional material that includes a list of exhibitors, also your company name, address, telephone, telex and facsimile number as well as a brief description of your business activities will be featured in the exhibition's catalogue. This catalogue will be given free or sold to fellow exhibitors and visitors and is usually only available at the exhibition or by request after it has taken place. Some exhibition organisers produce a catalogue in advance of the event, but this is not the norm. National and local press promotions will also be planned and press comment will be followed up with releases appearing in specialist trade papers and journals. Naturally, the organisers will request that you meet certain deadlines in order for your details to be included in the catalogue and as this is all part of the cost of renting your stand space it is worth meeting those deadlines.

Organisers of most major exhibitions provide an Exhibitions Order Book or Manual that not only gives you full details of the exhibition in relation to construction, site services etc, but also details of the press coverage and promotions that will occur, what promotion aids are available to the

Television interview at Hunting, Shooting and Fishing Show
Check with the organiser as to when they expect TV or radio. If you
have something of interest tell them, they often put a list together
for incoming TV and radio crews. You can also contact the media
direct – always worth doing as it could result in many thousands of
pounds' worth of free promotion.

exhibitor, when major trade press journal copy dates are etc.
Most professional organisers provide a number of order
forms at the back of the exhibition manual so all you have to
do is fill in your requirements. What site services do you
need? What and how many promotional or visitor attraction
aids (posters, stickers, leaflets, tickets) do you require? When
you return these forms to the organisers (sometimes the form
is sent by you direct to the appropriate contractor), your
request for material is processed and the facilities you
require on site will be supplied. Be sure to return the forms
by the date given to ensure that your orders are delivered on
time.

Using the marketing opportunities

For any exhibition or indeed any promotional campaign,
there are set aids that a business can use such as posters, corres-

pondence, stickers and multilingual visitor attraction leaflets. These are specifically produced promotional items which provide a valuable aid in getting the message across. Stickers are invariably printed with a slogan such as 'See us at . . .' or 'We'll be there' and the name of the exhibition, its dates and venue. The visitor attraction leaflets are usually multilingual for an international event and include full details about the exhibition and a comprehensive list of exhibitors, another reason for booking your stand early. It is useful from a PR point of view to be included in this list and as many organisers produce visitor attraction leaflets some six to eight months before an exhibition, you need to book early to gain maximum benefit from this exposure. Other pre-promotions arranged by the organisers may include overseas editors' visits. You could get to meet the editors of international trade publications and present your company and its products to them when they come over to preview the exhibition and see something of the industry the exhibition represents. If you are interested in overseas business and the organiser is arranging an inward mission of editors, make sure you are involved. In addition to promotion, you could well find that an editor has distributor contacts and valuable information about the likely interest there may be in your product in his or her country.

1   *Specialist advertisement*
    These advertisements are placed in pre-researched and pre-targeted publications in trade and technical areas. The advertisement, whatever its size, must relate specifically to the exhibition and be worded so that it attracts potential visitors already targeted;
2   *Direct mail*
    Direct mail should only be sent to previously targeted areas before the exhibition. The number mailed depends on (a) your budget and (b) your target potential. Many thousands of brochures and publications can be sent both in the UK and overseas. If attending a large international trade fair it might be worthwhile printing multilingual brochures and leaflets if you are keen to develop overseas business, and using these leaflets in your direct mail operation. Mailings to all relevant trade organisations, industrial and official bodies, Chambers of

Commerce, trade commissions and government information offices at home and overseas should also be carried out. It is important to reassess the type of mailing as the approach and the potential might differ;

3   *Press relations campaign*

Personal contact with local trade journal editors should be actively pursued in order to gain the widest possible press coverage. If you do not have anyone within your firm whose job scope enables them to produce an active and worthwhile campaign, then you will have to hire a well-known PR company;

4   *The exhibition organisers' press office*

Prior to and during the show the press office process exhibitors' information, news items and photographs and send these out in the form of press releases to national, local and specialist media and news agencies. These press releases are aimed at securing maximum editorial coverage of the exhibition and if you have a newsworthy story of your exhibit you should let them know. In most cases you will have to supply the press officer or publicity manager with press releases and photographs;

5   *Promotional facilities*

If attending an overseas or international trade fair, do ensure that you liaise with the Central Office of Information so that full advantage can be taken of their extensive overseas promotional facilities;

6   *Free tickets*

The exhibition organisers will supply you with a number of free tickets for your own distribution. Liaising with your fellow directors and managers, work out a suitable client 'hit list' and send complimentary tickets to them. You and your colleagues should be clear about what hospitality you will offer them when they arrive. Once they have accepted the invitation, make sure all stand staff know the names of who will be attending.

Invitations

The decision as to who is going to be invited to your stand must be taken by yourself and other senior managers. The organisers will give you a certain amount of complimentary tickets and in some cases badges, which will need careful allocation. Several months beforehand, draw up a guest list of overseas clients and send their invitations out in good time. Also draw up a list of UK clients, allowing yourself a lead time of three to four months. Organise some extra badges as invariably people will arrive having forgotten to bring their own. If replies have not been received from the invitees, a phone call is necessary to confirm your numbers – especially if catering is involved.

Extras

A promotional campaign aims to attract pre-targeted visitors to your stand. Its secondary aim is to attract exhibition visitors who may turn out to be valued customers at a later date.

To get the best possible value from your exhibition budget, you must ensure that your publicity person and your stand staff are fully aware of the visitor attraction programme planned for your stand. Depending upon the extent of your budget and promotional plans you could, for example, hire promotions girls or use existing staff to walk around the show handing out stickers or leaflets with an invitation to visit the stand to watch a specific demonstration. (Check first with

the organiser or consult the exhibition's rules and regulations, as some organisers do not allow this.) It is important
that your representatives are clearly identifiable, perhaps by
sashes or large lapel stickers.

A full parameter banner site has considerable impact and
will aid stand promotion. It will also help you and others
to identify the stand in busy exhibition halls. Banner sites
are usually placed strategically within multi-hall shows or
in the reception area of a single hall show. The banner can
have a slogan printed across it in full colour or simply
show your company's name in two colours with your stand
number.

Printed matter

Decide well in advance what printed matter you need. This
may take the form of additional leaflets, posters, visitor
attendance stickers, other stickers etc. What you decide upon
depends on your budget, your visitor target and the type of
exhibition you are attending.

Leaflets and brochures

Writing the text for a leaflet or brochure can be difficult and
it is important to have it expertly done. You may wish to
include details such as how long your company has been
established, its type of operation and the products offered.
Brochures/leaflets can be divided into two areas; company
brochures and product leaflets. Product leaflets include
specific ones on an item of machinery, which state what sort
of machine it is, the exact specification of that machine, its
capabilities and uses, and so on. Price lists may also be
needed for loose inserts into that literature.

How much literature you use on the stand is up to you and
your colleagues and what you feel will aid your sales.
Remember, however, cluttered stands are not appealing ones
and it is not always necessary to have leaflets on every sale-
able item. Correct ordering is important as if you run out of
leaflets not only are potential sales lost but from a management point of view it is highly embarrassing.

Participating in an overseas event means the translation of

leaflets and brochures. Professional translators should be hired, either from the Chambers of Commerce or from another reputable organisation. Your exhibition organisers will be able to put you in touch with the right people. As a guide, when deciding how many translations to obtain, check with the organisers as to the visitor profile. They will give you a breakdown of countries where visitors will be coming from. If it is a major international event, however, it is worth the expense of translating your material into all the major European languages.

Self-adhesive and other promotional stickers

Stickers are usually oblong but window stickers tend to be circular; both types have an adhesive area at the back. They can be printed in two colours or more. Usually a suitably catchy logo can be used and incorporated into the overall theme of your exhibition concept. Some exhibitors like to co-ordinate the theme of their stand with that of the exhibition or indeed throughout their printed matter and promotional activities. You can produce greater results simply because of continuity of approach.

Posters

Posters are another form of promotional aid that can be used within the display or as part of the shell systems. Permission has got to be gained, however, before they are used in other exhibition areas.

Advertising

If your budget allows, placing an advertistment in trade and technical publications may be a cost-effective use of promotional funds. Cost out the size of each advertisement, whether it is a quarter page, half page or a full page, whether or not you have to pay for special positions and what costs relate to full or partial colour or black and white.

Advertisements have visual impact and should be clear and uncluttered, directing the reader's eye directly to the message. The message can differ greatly and so, therefore, can the content and design. For a specialist advertisement in a targeted publications area attracting visitors, an invitation to visit the stand should be shown clearly on the advertisement with the stand number for ease of location. The placing of these advertisements needs to be carefully considered in the run up to the show. Should you advertise in the local or national press? Will the trade press collect all the necessary enquiries? Have you consulted with the organisers to establish what advertising activities are planned? Are any special features or previews planned by the media?

Saturating the press a week before the event generates a good response provided you have carefully selected the right media. Placing your advertisements at precise intervals will enhance the exposure.

Press releases

The major trade journals carry pre-exhibition articles, and usually feature a major preview during the time the exhibition is running, with review articles on how the exhibition and its attendants fared. Their reporters will be looking for stories that can generate interest and tie in with their articles. Press releases should, therefore, be written to coincide with this. They should also be written with the advertising campaign in mind so that duality of marketing purpose can be attained.

Press releases should be short in length, stating an interesting change, product, etc. The sentences need to be written in a punchy style and should not be ponderous either in length or subject. Usually releases extend to one A4 page but no

more than two. At the end of the release, it should clearly state who to contact for further information, the company's name, address, telephone and facsimile number as well as the stand number and location.

Press releases can also be sent out to customers, shareholders and retail suppliers. Again, clearly identify the date(s), location of the event and the stand number. If possible enclose an inviation; allow two tickets as most visitors to exhibitions come with a colleague.

Catalogues

Exhibition catalogues are another area where an invaluable reference to your stand can be made. These catalogues are not only in great demand during the exhibition but afterwards, as a point of reference.

As an exhibitor, your company details will be listed free of charge as well as the products you are displaying. As the information is supplied by yourself, make sure that both company and product details for any associates and principals exhibiting with you are included on the appropriate forms. These forms must be returned to the organisers by the closing date otherwise inclusion in the catalogue is not guaranteed. The impact is lost if late entries end up on addendum sheets.

As well as company lists, advertisements in these catalogues can prove a worthwhile marketing investment. Not only do they attract the visitors' attention to your presence, but they also endorse your marketing message and act as a useful reminder to a potential purchaser for many months after the show. This is an option and as such it depends mostly on the state of your budget.

As with other publications, special and prime positions in the catalogue cost more, and are normally booked well in advance. Check with the organisers' catalogue department as soon as possible.

Direct mail

When producing leaflets and brochures for the exhibition try to estimate as accurately as possible the number required not only for distribution at the exhibition but for pre-exhibition mailings. Remember, a rerun will be expensive, so it is better to have a few thousand left over to use later than have to print again.

In addition, consider what translated material will be needed as it will cut your costs per item if the literature is printed in the same run. A further consideration is the size and weight of the leaflets to be printed as the paper weight could increase your postage cost. Consider also what is to be included in the mailing, i.e. an offer of free tickets to attend, etc. In all likelihood you will have to go to a direct mailing house in order to distribute unless you have the facilities within your business. Mail houses cost out mailings on a thousand envelopes mailed basis.

To ensure you are getting to the right target audience, ask the mail house how often they 'clean' their list. What is the accuracy of the mailing? How often is this list in use? All-in packages can be offered by these mail houses or you can purchase the list and do it yourself.

Some exhibition organisers have a corporate database mailing which is available to exhibitors and assists in pre-show target mailings. The exhibitor can select from an extensive list of previous visitors. The categories are broken down (as with other mailing house listings) as follows:

1 Company classification;
2 Geographical location;
3 Product interest;
4 Position with the firm.

This can complement and become a cost-effective addition to your own in-house list.

Whatever pre-show promotion you decide upon, its duty is to inform, remind and promote prospects to visit your stand.

Always keep the organisers' PR office fully informed of any news concerning your products or activities relevant to your participation at the exhibition as they may be able to include items in their regular press communications.

Stand staff

This area is covered comprehensively in Chapter 5, but as an addendum to stand promotion must also be mentioned here. The sales team and the stand staff must be properly briefed as soon as the event is planned and thereafter kept regularly informed with regard to the exhibition, the products on the stand and any special events. Select a team to work on the stand and brief them on the existing customers and suppliers who have agreed to visit. It is important that a co-ordinated approach is used by all stand staff and this can only be successfully accomplished by thorough briefing. Time and money sensibly spent on co-ordinating promotional campaigns go a long way towards maximising the unique marketing opportunity available at exhibitions.

5

The human factor

Advance planning and thorough briefing of members of staff who are to attend the exhibition is essential. Not only do they have to know the purpose of the exhibition and the potential for better business it can bring the company, they need to know the finer points such as who has been specially invited to attend, any specialist design areas, products, product launches or demonstrations. This applies whether you are participating in a consumer or trade fair.

The number of staff chosen to man the exhibition stand must be carefully considered, based upon the size of the stand, number of demonstrations and so on. Overmanning creates a stand with a cluttered, disorganised appearance, whilst undermanning leaves a staff shortage that can result in lost sales.

Exhibitions can be physically demanding on staff as they are on their feet in an enclosed environment for long periods of the day. The atmosphere is an artificially created one and can be physically draining. Loss of attention can occur after only a few hours, and by the end of the day, feet can be sore and tempers frayed. Mentally, the resultant problems can be lack of attention to detail in demonstrating equipment, failure to close a sale etc.

Set up a staff roster whereby two people man the stand for a set period of time, whilst two others can rest and relieve the stand staff later. Numbers may vary, but you should have no less than two manning the stand at any given time. It is worth considering an incentive package for your in-house staff if they are going to man your stand, particularly if they are expected to work throughout the event. Most exhibitions are staged in interesting cities or towns like London for example,

and many of your staff will want to take advantage of the opportunity to see a show or go 'on the town'. While you cannot dictate what your staff do in their own time it is advisable to ensure that everyone gets a good night's sleep while working on the stand. Make it clear that the exhibition is very important to the company and that any 'zombies' that appear on the stand after a night on the town will be sent home. The incentive package could include a night out for your staff after the exhibition closes.

Determine the number and status of your stand staff as soon as possible. Ask them whether they are willing to work on the stand. Set a day or more aside before the exhibition when you can run a briefing session on how the staff are to appear and behave on the stand. If you are having uniforms specially made then they must be advised on these and where to go to obtain them. You must also make arrangements with regard to payment once agreement has been reached as to who will attend. Advise them of the dates they will have to be on the stand by using a roster system; also circulate the times as well as transportation arrangements to and from the exhibition.

Always book hotel accommodation well in advance. There have been cases not long after the NEC opened near Birmingham when stand staff had to make do with accommodation as far away as Nottingham. Late booking means little or no choice of accommodation or having to pay a premium in a lower class of accommodation or an inconvenient location. This can cause your budget to overshoot as well as adversely affecting staff morale.

If you have to cancel rooms already booked, a cancellation charge might be due, so be absolutely certain of the number of rooms needed for the duration of the event. Hotel accommodation booking agents can be approached if you want advance block booking and you have little time to chase preferential rates and adequate accommodation.

Client hospitality during the exhibition may necessitate dinner bookings being made. Here it is worthwhile choosing one restaurant well beforehand and booking a table for six to eight people for five nights 'starting from and ending with' and then confirming the exact numbers two weeks before the exhibition starts.

Stand manager's role

In most cases in small businesses, the stand manager will be you. The role played by the stand manager will be to oversee this event from start to finish; organising, planning and attending it, and making all the decisions.

To assist you in your duties you should appoint an assistant who will help co-ordinate the events and make sure that everything runs as smoothly as possible. He or she will have the responsibility of making decisions in your absence.

As the exhibition progresses so the stand manager's role changes. You have a responsibility to the visitors to the stand (especially existing clients) to make sure that their enquiries are taken care of. Security and safe keeping of equipment is also under your control.

Think of your exhibition stand as an extension of your own premises, which because of the nature of the exhibition or show is open to public view. It follows that stand staff and representatives of your company are on public view also. Impressions gained by the stand visitors are created by you and your staff. A bad impression will affect your business.

Stand staff will meet not only visitors who require technical information, but also senior decision makers who may be potential customers. As such they must be fully versed on the company and the products. Their attitude must be positive. Undermanning is as bad as overmanning. Many members of staff milling around will give the impression that the company has had few visitors and no enquiries. Undermanning of a stand, on the other hand, can cause serious problems; if visitors are not attended to the loss of potential sales could result.

After selecting your most personable and knowledgeable staff, set a day aside when all members of staff concerned with the event can be present for a briefing session. Go through the location of the exhibition and its facilities if possible, the position of the stand, what will be on it, who to contact in case of problems, details of the staff roster, and company policy and products. Any details pertaining to the stand or your company's presence at the exhibition must be given to the stand staff. Lastly, make sure they know how to meet and address clients (see page 55).

If you cannot be present on the day or days of the exhibition, then you must appoint a stand manager early on in the planning stage. This person will take the day-to-day responsibility for the stand. If you have to appoint a stand manager for whatever reason, the person should be fully briefed on the company's objectives at the outset of the decision to participate at the exhibition. This person should also have a say in selecting the stand staff. Naturally, when you come to appoint the individual you will do so because they have certain management and personnel skills which will enable them not only to plan but also to handle any difficult situation that could arise.

The stand manager should decide what facilities to have on the stand, such as a coffee-making machine or wine, and also if the staff should wear a company uniform. This uniform can consist of simply a certain style and colour of jacket or extend to a full blown co-ordinated outfit, which of course is likely to be expensive. If the decision goes against uniforms the stand manager should make sure that all staff are appropriately and smartly dressed. Women are advised not to wear high heels at an exhibition to avoid aching feet.

Selecting stand staff

As the stand staff are your company's ambassadors, they should be well versed in your company aims and products. Staff selection is critical, and should take place well beforehand so that staff can be fully briefed on all details, including where they are staying and how they are to get to the exhibition. The stand manager will have created a roster and each member of staff should be given a copy.

When selecting staff to attend the exhibition you should break down their expertise into four categories; sales, promotions, technical and miscellaneous (obviously, for the consumer show this will differ). Small businesses might find that they have a category of indivudals who perhaps perform two or more tasks, e.g. sales, administration and miscellaneous. Select two from each category so that one will be manning the stand while the other is resting. They should know who existing clients are and be competent in attracting new ones.

You might have hired a promotional person to handle your exhibition promotion. If that is the case, this person should attend the exhibition to deal with any media enquiries or any promotional problems that might arise. Technical specialists should also be available. Enquiries will always be made for more technical information. If this information is not available then you should ensure that at least one technician is contactable at the office by telephone throughout the exhibition so that any questions can be answered. Stand staff, irrespective of their seniority within the firm from managing director down to office clerk, must have sufficient background information on the company's products to work on the stand on a day-to-day basis. They should know whether to pass a visitor on to the salesman or to a technician. Visitor hospitality must also be looked after by stand staff.

Four or more staff should be available on a day-to-day basis. Every three or four hours they should be given a break, with regular drinks throughout the day as the atmosphere in exhibitions can become dry and stuffy. Staff cannot be expected to remain alert from 9 in the morning to 7 in the evening. In order to keep stand staff efficient and thus effective, they should be able to get away from the stand to sit down and rest their feet, and have a cup of coffee if necessary.

One of the stand manager's duties is to ensure that the stand is kept tidy at all times. For example, briefcases should not be kept on the stand but stored out of sight. Newspapers and books should not be allowed on the stand either, the only literature allowed should be the sales and company promotional literature. Eating and drinking on the stand should not be permitted unless it is in the hospitality area. Smoking should not be allowed, except by visitors. However, ashtrays should be placed on tables for use by visitors and emptied regularly.

These rules and regulations should be handed out in written form to all those manning the stands, as their help and co-operation is essential. Details given to staff should include:

- Stand information, including map of the exhibition noting toilets, rest rooms, organisers' office, telephones;
- Duty rosters;
- Accommodation and transportation arrangements;
- Company information with regard to products;

- Details of uniform or standard of dress;
- Any special demonstrations;
- Hospitality arrangements, a copy of the exhibition catalogue with a list of other exhibitors. Visitors are likely to
  ask about the times of various functions in the show, and
  it is good PR if your staff can help them. Most of this
  information will be in the catalogue;
- Any company promotions and special events held during
  the exhibition along with any literature;
- List of all known visitors who will attend as well as any
  senior members of staff, e.g. company chairman;
- Special enquiry forms to be filled in and kept in a safe
  place;
- A list of all stand housekeeping duties; (a) a stand must be
  left tidy each evening, all literature must be replenished;
  (b) any literature that is dirty or dog-eared must be
  removed; (c) always ensure that there is an adequate supply of writing materials so that orders or further information can be noted on the enquiry forms, and so on;
- Catering requirements must also be noted but it must be
  stressed that any 'extras' ordered need the stand manager's approval;
- Daily sales should be given to the stand manager for safe
  keeping;
- The stand manager and his assistant are usually stand key
  holders so they should be the first to arrive in the morning and the last to leave at night. Punctuality is important.

At the end of each day, the stand manager or his assistant
should de-brief stand staff back at the hotel. All sales leads
achieved throughout the day should be passed to the manager
who must keep them secure or send them back to the office.

Questions must be asked, such as did any problems arise?
How many visitors came to the stand? (This figure can also
be found by counting the entries in the visitors book.) Ask
the staff whether or not they were able to cope and were any
actual sales made.

Stand staff briefing

If new products are to be launched at the exhibition, then
their functions and mechanics should be explained fully. If

display equipment of any sort is to be used then the staff must be shown how to use it.

Training videos for stand staff can be hired from Video Arts Limited in London. These videos are useful as part of a company's one-day training programme. There are many more duties in successfully manning a stand than at first spring to mind and as such, you should train your staff in certain niceties. Below is a list of DOs and DON'Ts.

DO

- Offer a friendly smile;
- Leave visitors for a few minutes to wander around;
- Approach and make a suitable remark such as 'Have you used our machinery? Have you seen our brochure on . . . ?'
- Ask the visitor who he works for and what his role is;
- Make sure that further information is given;
- Wear your company badge;
- Speak to everyone who comes to the stand;
- Give people sufficient time to read particular items of interest;
- Be friendly. If busy dealing with an existing visitor, smile or nod to acknowledge the new visitor;
- Introduce visitors to the relevant members of your company. Not only by name but by title as well.

DON'T

- Rush over to visitors, let them come on to the stand;
- Stand chatting in corners with other staff members;
- Sit around smoking or drinking coffee;
- Leave visitors unattended for any length of time;
- Say 'Can I help you?' – ask open-ended questions;
- Promise to send literature and forget to write out an enquiry slip;
- Stand arms folded across your chest glaring at visitors;
- Stand with other staff in groups;
- Stand in a position blocking access to the stand;
- Sit and read newspapers;
- Make visitors feel they are a nuisance. The stand staff should always look enthusiastic; sales can get lost through staff pouncing as visitors come on to a stand or leaving them to their own devices.

Stand staff should fill in enquiry forms of each contact made including name and address, position held and nature of enquiry. The position that this person holds in the company is important as decision makers are potential buyers. If any further information is needed, then this should be noted on the enquiry form so that it can be sent out at a later date. All enquiry forms must be collected and kept in a safe place. By using this system, additional sales can be made. The list builds itself up, the company's information on visitors' awareness and needs expands, and news of future products to be launched can be mailed to this list.

Other areas

Punctuality

Stand staff must be aware of the exhibition's opening and closing times. It is the duty of the stand manager to ensure that the stand is manned at all times. Staff should be there half an hour before the exhibition opens, preparing the stand. Before leaving at night, the stand should be tidied. There is nothing more unprofessional than a stand laden with overflowing ashtrays and dirty cups, and should the key-holder be late one morning and the stand left untidy from the previous day, this can occur. Such an image can be harmful. Always ensure that there are at least two keyholders if the stand is enclosed or has a hospitality suite or office.

Handling visitors

Role play sessions should be organised so that the stand staff know where to place themselves on the stand, how to strike up a conversation with people, how to ascertain whether or not the visitor is genuinely interested and a potential client. They should practise how to ask open-ended questions.

Hospitality

The facilities you provide for your visitors should comple-ment your activities. However, hospitality can be very expensive. In order for it to be cost-effective, it must be targeted and properly controlled. If you are entertaining on your stand, then you should have a separate area panelled off. Hospitality should be restricted to this area leaving the stand as a showcase for visitors. People standing around your display area chatting over beer and sandwiches will disrupt sales enquiries, putting off any new potential customers. Hospitality should be for the customer's benefit. The stand organiser or manager should know who to invite in and when. After all, it is a facility where business can be discussed and business contracts made in a relaxed atmosphere. It is not a resting place for freeloaders or stand staff.

If large groups of visitors are envisaged then it might be worthwhile renting a hospitality suite at the exhibition hall. This frees your stand space and stand staff so that they can concentrate on fulfilling their main role. It also helps you keep a closer eye on entertaining costs.

Some special customers may need to be entertained in the evening. When pre-planning the event, select a suitable restaurant and book a table well in advance. Confirm a few weeks before the start of the exhibition the exact number for dinner each night.

You have a number of choices when deciding on the level of hospitality:

- Coffee and tea facilities;
- Soft drinks and beer/wine;
- Liquor, wine, soft drinks;
- Snacks such as crisps, peanuts etc;
- Sandwiches and other snacks with wine, beer etc;
- Sit-down lunches/dinners;
- Breakfast meetings.

Again, consult your budget. Will the type of entertainment chosen enhance your exhibition aims? Whatever route you decide on, plan and order well beforehand. If liquor is kept on the stand, then make sure each evening it is securely locked away.

If a hospitality area is part of the stand, glasses and coffee cups should be washed up each evening and put away so that everything is left neat and tidy. For major cleaning tasks, the exhibition organisers will be able to help. The venue's catering order office will be able to assist should catering supplies be needed.

As the organisers know the area around the exhibition, it is worth consulting them before making any restaurant bookings or catering arrangements. Hospitality can be a valuable resource in ensuring an exhibition's success.

Security

Stand security it vitally important. There have been occasions where displays have been tampered with, liquor has gone missing, names and addresses of leads have been 'misplaced' and so on. Each day the stand staff will be busy dealing with visitors, taking down new contact names and addresses for future sales or leads. This list, by the end of the exhibition, represents potential income and as such is valuable. Industrial espionage can take many forms. Competitors might go to considerable lengths to get hold of such information, and so these forms need to be kept in a secure place.

Stand security can be put in jeopardy when a stand is unmanned. The stand manager should ensure that the stand includes a cupboard which has a secure lock. All liquor should be locked away. Portable valuables should be removed each evening and taken back to the hotel to be locked up in the hotel safe. Beware of leaving valuables in a locked office; access can usually be a simple matter, particularly if there is no roof.

Normally the stand manager is responsible for security on the stand during the open hours of an exhibition and the organisers or hall owners take over when the exhibition is closed. Thefts can and do happen so pay particular attention to valuable items; the worst time is after the exhibition closes and the breakdown of the stands begins. Be sure to remove all moveable items at the first possible moment. Breakdown at an exhibition can become a free for all and this is when even the best security fails.

Stand security also entails looking after displays. If these are mobile then security guards should be recruited. Remember, whatever equipment is on the stand, it must conform to the health and safety standards. Most importantly, remember also to arrange adequate insurance cover.

6

Pre-exhibition timetable and checklist

Working on a twelve-month planning cycle, this chapter deals with all the jobs that should be done before the exhibition begins. Your own timetable may vary. You may use a six or eight-month cycle or indeed for large international shows the calendar may be eighteen months to two years. Within this time you will fix tasks, follow through on decisions, convene meetings, inspect and check all tenders, production, stand design and construction and deal with the day-to-day administrative work that planning and organising an exhibition entails. These tasks are so numerous and varied that the best thing to do is draw up a simple schedule.

Stand content

What goes on the stand varies from exhibitor to exhibitor, from exhibition to exhibition and from trade fair to consumer exhibition. A checklist will be of use when deciding on the final content of your stand.

Checklist - stand content

- Brochures
- Leaflets
- Product sample
- Promotional gifts
- Telephone
- List of services

- Business cards
- Press releases
- Press packages
- Visitors book
- Catering arrangements
- Files: Sales
          Catering/accommodation
          Miscellaneous
- Enquiry forms
- Pens/pencils
- Notebooks
- List of exhibits
- Exhibition equipment
- Audio-visual aids
- Banners
- Photographic display panels
- Badges
- Flowers/pot plants
- Furniture
- Beverages
- Materials
- Snacks
- List of useful addresses for taxis, restaurants, etc.

It is important to ensure that all the appropriate above items are packed away at the end of the day in a secure locker. The key holder's name should be given to each member of staff. Replacing the equipment is expensive, so when transporting these items to the exhibition (probably in the boots of staff cars), check in items when being packed and check them out again at the other end.

Product samples and gifts

As part of your marketing strategy you may have certain product samples to give away. Usually, there is some form of promotional gift that is attached to the sample. These gifts vary from pens or notepads to more expensive items. The company's name and logo as well as the address and telephone number is usually reproduced on each time. If these gift packages are available then you should ensure that you have enough for the entire exhibition and that the staff know the level of distribution. In all likelihood, there will be more visitors on the first day than the last day and so in order not to run out, daily monitoring should be done.

In addition to product samples and promotional gifts you will also be giving out literature on your product or services. Literature is expensive to produce and should not be wasted. Visiting exhibitions, you will see people walking around with their arms full of paper which at the end is placed in the waste paper bin. Stand staff should be made aware of the available literature and the quantity for distribution. No company wants to go away with a pile of paper of no relevance once the exhibition is over. But equally, no one wants to reprint expensive brochures for the last two days of the exhibition.

There should be two levels of literature given out, a comprehensive all-in brochure for the more serious sales enquiries and an inexpensive one to give away to casual visitors. Product samples and promotional gifts should not be handed out freely either. It is important to make your stand staff aware of the cost and relevance of these items. Normally, there is a corporate brochure listing the services/products provided, the existence of the company policies. If display machinery is on the stand, there should be leaflets giving details of specifications on each of the products displayed. In addition, if a new product is going to be launched, then there should be a leaflet/brochure on it. When leaflets are given out to stand visitors it is important to ensure that a business card is attached to the main brochure. Enquiries may be made months or years after the exhibition date by visitors who have retained the card but thrown away the brochure. If you are going to exhibit on a regular basis, it would be worthwhile printing a card which can identify when it was given out. A key code can be used by placing a number in a bracket in the left-hand corner at the bottom of the card. The code could be 89/ (identifying the year) 9/ (identifying the month) O (identifying the venue, in this case Olympia).

Recording information

Anyone coming on to the stand should be asked to sign a visitors book. This is not possible on each occasion, but if not then a business card should be asked for so that this information can be processed.

When ordering your literature, you might find it useful to have a simple enquiry form printed so that the stand staff can fill these in during the exhibition. They can then be filed in the appropriate file on a daily basis. If notes are taken, then these together with all sales leads should be duplicated and kept in a safe place. One large company employed two secretaries so that at the end of every day, names and addresses of stand visitors could be typed out on sticky labels. The literature was then sent to visitors. These labels were duplicated and the second copy was returned to the sales director for his retention. A light pen can do this via a computer data bank.

Other back-up information might be needed on the stand, including price lists, product delivery times etc.

If technical staff cannot be available on the stand, then all information should be available for visitors' enquiries. It is also good policy to arrange for a technical member of staff to be available back at the office to answer any queries. However, should you have equipment on display, then it is essential to have at least one technician on the stand.

Demonstrations

Demonstrations can range from a moving piece of machinery to an audio-visual display of the equipment. These demonstrations vary from trade to consumer shows. In the latter, individuals may form part of the demonstration.

In purpose-built exhibition halls like the NEC space is available for large pieces of equipment, such as newspaper printing presses; even earth-moving vehicles can be driven in through the NEC access doors, and working exhibits are more common now. Static exhibits or mock-ups, though not as impressive as working ones, can be used as part of an eye-catching display. If mobile demonstrations are used, then you should plan set times during the course of the day when these will be run. Stand staff members can tour the hall giving out invitations if this is allowed. (Small events might allow this but most do not. The same applies for distribution of literature; it is usually only allowed from the stand.) If a working demonstration of a piece of equipment is to be used then you must ensure that proper safeguards for safety are installed. Barriers need to be erected. Not only can visitors have accidents, but the machines can be tampered with by competitors. Equipment on display must conform to the health and safety standards. Permission for its use must also have been gained from the organisers. Make sure you have adequate insurance cover in case of accidents.

During a working display, sufficient stand staff should be available to handle enquiries and to give out literature. On these occasions, it is likely that the number of visitors to your stand will increase considerably.

Demonstrations should be kept to four to six each day. Frequent demonstrations lessen the overall impact. If audiovidual equipment is being used, be sure to have back-up information slides should any of them become damaged. Use of audio-visual aids can be quite controversial should the volume be too loud or the screen affect surrounding stands. Other exhibitors may be using the same type of equipment for the same objectives. The result is a cataclysm of sound. Remember, if the display causes a nuisance to

either other stands or to the overall exhibition then the organisers have the right to close down the stand. At the very least you could waste valuable exhibition sales time sorting out a dispute.

There are many types of audio-visual equipment on the market and it is worthwhile consulting the experts six months or so before the exhibition. As part of your stand design you should decide what type of equipment to use (if any) and where to hire it from. Visual displays can be used on a screen. If using slide equipment then do make sure that each slide is numbered and placed in the carousel in the correct order. Duplicate slides can be held in reserve should a slide become distorted.

Cyclic events

There are many exhibitions that occur annually or biannually. Some of these are well-attended consumer shows, such as the Motor Show, Royal Show etc. Others come under the heading of trade fairs. Whatever category they come under, space can be booked a year or more in advance. For example, Hotelympia – The International Hotel and Catering exhibition – is held every two years at Olympia, London in January. Hospitality – The National Hotel and Catering exhibition – is held at the National Exhibition Centre in Birmingham in January in the non-Hotelympia year. The Laundry exhibition at the NEC occurs only every six years and runs in a cycle of exhibitions that are staged in France and Germany every two years, i.e. Laundry UK, NEC 1988, Germany 1990, France 1992 than back to NEC in 1994. Most exhibitions are annual, every two years or every three years.

Countdown checklist

Month Number	Duty	Action
12	Decision to exhibit	Advise advertising agency
	Appoint exhibition organising manager and assistant	Advise relevant staff
	Select site, prepare budget, reserve site	Gain all relevant details from exhibition organisers
	Reserve staff accommodation	
	Check availability of hospitality suites at venue	
11	Brief stand designers	Appoint stand designer
		Agree product display and brief designer
10	Receive stand design	Approve stand design
9	Prepare special exhibits	Order displays and any products to be made
7	Submit plans to organisers	Gain approval from organisers
6	Tender to be placed with stand contractors	Select contractor
	Brief advertising/ publicity agency/ assistant	Plan advertising and publicity campaign
		Back-up advertising

Month Number	Duty	Action
5	Check auxiliary services such as air, plumbing and fitments	Place your requirements with organisers, e.g. electricity, water and compressed air, plumbing and fitments
	Prepare initial press release	Send initial press release
	Agree back-up advertising	Place back-up advertising
	Stand literature, exhibition and technical brochures	Check copy for accuracy
	Arrange photographic sessions for press release and brochure copy	Develop same
	Arrange translations	Check and agree translated copy
	Order stand furniture, flowers	Confirm order
	Brief copywriter	Check his/her work
4	Arrange stand insurance, cleaning; confirm accommodation	Confirm same in writing
	Approve working details	Brief all relevant staff members
	Order typesetting of literature	Check proofs
	Liaise with members of staff re guest list	Prepare guest list
	Advertising copy for exhibition catalogue and for second stage of advertisements	Place advertisement

Month Number	Duty	Action
3	Plan staff requirements	Check with staff whether approved
	Arrange hospitality events, place bookings	
	Decide number of tickets and badges	Order same
	Prepare second press release	Send second press release
	Prepare ticket despatch	Send tickets
	Check stand construction	
	Check prefabrication	
	Check transport needed	
	Send copy of exhibition leaflets to printers	Await proofs
2	Check delivery of printed material	Check printed material
	Check security element	Make arrangements if necessary
	Check assembly of stand, amend if necessary	
	Arrange staff roster	
	Prepare third press release	Send third press release
	Arrange press reception	Send invitations
	Arrange photographer	Confirm same
	Send tickets and invitations	

Month Number	Duty	Action
	Check advertising/ further literature	
	Check site machinery	Run machinery in
	Prepare staff training programme	Book suitable date
	Double check all arrangements	
	Confirm staff uniforms	Purchase uniforms
	Insurance cover	Check policy and instigate insurance cover
1	Brief staff	
	Confirm final arrangements for press and final arrangements for reception	
	Prepare press packs and send out final pre-exhibition press release	
	Construct stand	Check everything that should have been ordered is ordered and machinery running
	Pre-exhibition run through with staff	
	On the day, hold reception	Assess reception
	Sales leads	Debrief staff
	Dismantle stand	Retain any parts for further use
	Check sales leads	Assess success

7

The build-up – what to expect

The atmosphere during the build-up to an exhibition is often one of excitement. Many of your colleagues will be experiencing a feeling of elation while others may experience a feeling of apprehension. This is where pre-planning and preparing a checklist comes into its own as it gives you the confidence that all that could have been done has been done.

If possible, it is better for you and your colleagues to arrive the day before the exhibition starts so that all of you can feel fresh and relaxed on the opening day. Some members of your team might decide to stay up and have a late night drink. They must be told that this is not advisable as their performance on the day will be marred. There is very little for you to do with regard to the construction of the stand except to ensure that everything has been done. If cannot be there, then your assistant should check to make sure that the equipment has arrived, your company's technician has set it up and that everything is in its place and working properly. Your file with contracts and letters of confirmation etc. should be taken to the exhibition. Should problems occur, it is useful to have them to hand.

The stand contractor will have erected all items on your stand in the position agreed and to the design specification given. The contractor will have organised the setting up of the electrics and lights and the waste system. Should a problem arise either through an oversight or a technical problem the best person to ask for help would be a representative from the exhibition organisers' office.

Who can help you on site

Depending upon the type of event, its construction can take from one day to ten days. The norm is usually four or five days. The larger consumer events take the longest build-up time. It is no use going to the event before your stand is ready. The organisers of the exhibition will have on site a reception staff, technical staff and organising manager as well as promotional staff. They are all there to help you and can and should be used. The organising staff will assist in giving out information, obtaining new badges, last-minute bookings or arrangements and so on. The exhibition organisers will distribute admission passes and details of car parking allocation. Usually these are sent out in advance or obtained from the organisers' office. Advice on off-loading and on-loading exhibition equipment to relevant loading bays has to be gained from this office also.

The organisers will have a visitor enquiry service in the reception room in the lobby of the central hall. They will

have details of all the exhibitors and be able to guide visitors to the appropriate stand.

The organising office supervises the overall event and will help you on such matters as supplies to your stand, amendment to any structural problem and so on.

The press officer for the exhibition organises pre-exhibition publicity and goes on arranging whatever PR or promotional exercises are planned throughout the exhibition. He or she organises press visits for the relevant media. You and your products could be of interest but it must be remembered that you are racing for editorial coverage and thus space. Being well prepared with any new product launch date, press release and appropriate literature is essential. You might feel that a special visit to your stand is called for to show off a new piece of equipment. It is important to establish good relations with the press officer or publicity manager at an early stage.

The benefits of establishing early on a good relationship with both the organising manager and his press office were seen at an Ideal Home Exhibition held at the NEC. On this occasion, the press were more interested in the delays and inconvenience caused by the air traffic controllers' strike at the adjacent airport. Quick thinking by the exhibition's PR manager not only gave nightly TV and national press coverage to the event but also allowed exhibitors to participate. To relieve congestion at the airport, the organisers laid on a shuttle service to bring families with small children to the show from the airport. Some were put up in show homes overnight while they waited for their flight to be called. The result was a massive press story showing on nationwide TV screens the scene of these families being housed and fed by exhibitors, with their products and company names viewed by millions. This sort of thing can happen at any time and it proves that if you have a good working relationship with the PR or publicity manager you can quickly take advantage of promotional opportunities when they occur.

Rules and regulations

Typical rules regarding your rights as an exhibitor are noted in this section. It is important to observe these rules because if you do not, as a final resort your stand can be closed down.

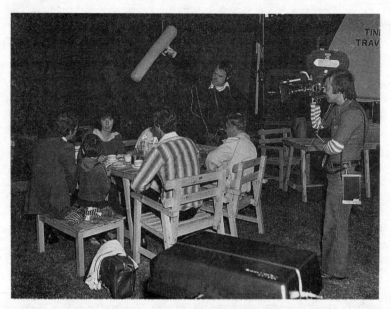

Family being interviewed by Central Television after staying the night in a show home. A host of exhibitors, including the builder, achieved national and provincial media coverage.

These rules regarding construction and erection of a stand are laid down by the organisers and are subject to the Health and Safety at Work Act, local building and fire regulations. Any stand of two-storey construction must be agreed with the organisers.

Electrical installation can only be carried out by the electricians appointed by the exhibition site organisers. Exceptions are sometimes made where specialised equipment is involved but all contractors must be members of an appropriate trade union. If lights are used on the fascia boards, then they should be only of sufficient power to light that board and not to cause any inconvenience to neighbouring stands. The organiser reserves the right to omit flashing lights, lasers and other electrical equipment.

Exhibitors cannot canvass visitors from general gangways without permission.

The exhibitor must keep his stand open and manned throughout the exhibition's opening hours. Official admission passes will be given to the exhibitor beforehand.

If the exhibitor or his staff causes damage to any of the other exhibitors' stands or to the exhibition building, then he must pay for any damage. The exhibitor is responsible for personal injury or damage to the property arising from either the erection or dismantling of the stand. The exhibitor must carry adequate insurance cover. All materials used in the display must not be flammable, dangerous or explosive.

Gangways in front of each exhibition stand must not be obstructed. Exhibits that are moving, i.e. not static, should not cause too much noise or annoyance to other exhibitors or visitors and must be installed and protected to the satisfaction of the organisers. Health and safety regulations have to be observed. Machines can be removed if these requisites are not met. Display equipment such as audio-visual aids can only be used with prior permission from the organisers and must not cause a nuisance to other exhibitors.

The exhibitor must ensure that his stand is kept in a clean and tidy state throughout the exhibition, although the stand is usually cleaned by the official cleaning contractor.

The stand must be taken down by the dates specified in the contract and all equipment removed from the premises. Should the organisers have to remove these items then any cost incurred for removal and storage of the exhibits will have to be met by the exhibitor.

The exhibition

On the opening day of the exhibition you may wish to arrange a special open day press reception. The open day is often also termed a press day as it is usually the day the press and dignitaries come in great numbers. Special press packages including the appropriate press releases along with company literature should be available in a press pack. Usually 50 copies will suffice, accompanied by six photographs for display in the press office with back-up copies of the photographs for the press on request. A similar amount should be supplied to the exhibition press centre.

The exhibition organisers usually have a press reception or luncheon and an opportunity can arise to mingle with members of the press and to talk to them about your own specific product. Trade publications usually publish articles pre-

A well-known face helping to attract visitors at an NEC exhibition.

exhibition, during the exhibition and directly afterwards. Some publications actually part-sponsor the events.

The first day of the exhibition is not always the busiest from an attendance point of view but is often the most important day in relation to press and the quality of visitors. Your company may wish to organise a special event. You could invite a personality to visit your stand if you really want to capture attention. Some companies have a special event on each day of the exhibition when selected customers and members of the press are invited. This can take place in the hospitality section of the stand or at pre-booked rooms in the hall. These events can be beneficial provided they are properly organised and that all concerned know of the event. Attendance at any press event is always a bit difficult to estimate, as if another event of greater importance or with a well-known person takes place at the same time as yours, then press numbers will be down. So check the organisers' daily diary of events and avoid conflicting with other events or receptions.

New product launches

An exhibition is a perfect place to launch a new product. Open day ceremonies coupled with a new product launch can be cost-effective and beneficial promotionally. If a new product is going to be launched on the stand and working displays are to be used, then ensure that they have been fully tested and working before the event. A machine or appliance that does not work when it is meant to can not only cause embarrassment and loss of credibility, it could cost you dearly in lost sales.

8

Evaluating performance

Deciding whether or not your exhibition stand has been successful can only be achieved by evaluating the results; debriefing staff, interpreting the organisers' post-exhibition statistics, following up your own sales leads and assessing expenditure. At the end, you will find out whether your objectives have been met by being at the event.

Exhibitions are often judged purely on a cost accounting basis. The true outcome can often be coloured by this. But what value can be placed on new sales? What value can be placed on encouraging continued customer loyalty? And what about the PR exposure?

Immediate evaulation is often not possible because sales contacts made can be slow in becoming clients. This assessment is best left until all the facts can be established. It does help considerably, however, if each evening during the exhibition, the stand manager debriefs staff to find out what happened during the course of that day. There might have been more visitors to the stand, for example, while sales contacts might be reduced. A potential client might have wanted specialist attention and needed further information.

The evaluation of a successful exhibition goes hand in hand with the meeting of its objectives. It is the assessment of any benefits gained. Every item of information is needed to make this assessment.

Naturally, certain objectives are easier to assess than others. For example, if your objective is achieving 100 sales leads and 50 direct sales then it is a relatively simple exercise. The difficulty arises when you have many objectives and some of them can be called imponderables. For example, how do you assess the increase in customer loyalty gained from attending the show? Is it a pure cost accounting one based on new orders received from them or does it go further? This chapter will look at certain objectives and their analysis.

The efficient organising of an exhibition will help when assessing its success. It is important that the stand manager gets a true overall view of the day-to-day situations that have occurred on his stand. So, at the end of an exhibition, once the exhibits have been packed away safely and the immediate pressure is off, the manager must thoroughly debrief the staff back at 'home base'. Do not try to get it done all at once; allow time for people to ponder on events, for potential orders to be followed up, and any post promotional activities to be carried out.

Debriefing staff

This debriefing can be done in two ways. The first is on a one-to-one basis whereby you assess one person's reaction to the event. Decide the questions and put them in a question-

naire. Each person will answer the same question differently, seeing the event from a different perspective. By circulating the questionnaire to all stand staff, you will be able to assess more easily the reactions and views gained.

The second takes the form of a group debriefing session, when all the stand staff are gathered and asked about their evaluation of the exhibition, the stand, the results, and so on. However, not everyone comes forward at these sessions so you might not get the volume of reaction that you would from debriefing on a one-to-one basis. The latter, of course, is more time-consuming. You can, however, adopt both methods and perhaps have a group session but send out questionnaires beforehand so that you can gain a greater depth of opinion.

Questions to aid your debriefing sessions are listed below:

1 What proportion of the stand's visitors wanted sales information? What form did it take (i.e. leaflets, further meetings, technical assessments, etc.)?
2 What is your overall opinion of the stand's presentation?
3 Could the stand design be improved?
4 Were any direct sales made? If so, on what models or service?
5 Was the amount of literature sufficient?
6 Were more individual items of literature needed, say, one per product?
7 Were the facilities at the exhibition sufficient? If not, what facilities could be improved upon?
8 Were competitors' stands better than our own? If so in what way?
9 What was the level of enquiries?
10 What would you like to see changed from the overall stand display?
11 Were the site amenities good?

Analysing sales and promotional results

When first deciding whether or not to exhibit, actual targeted sales results will have been outlined and other benefits raised, from promotional achievements to product launches. Previous results from other promotional/advertising/sales campaigns (possibly even exhibitions) if available will make it easier to formulate a comparison. For exhibitors who do not have a parallel to draw information from, then the exercise becomes more difficult. Also, as previously stated, some objectives are more difficult to assess than others. Promotional advantages might not be seen as immediate or indeed they could have merged with another promotional campaign currently being run by you. Sales leads might take time to come to fruition.

Checklist – sales achievements

Draw up your own checklist when determining the sales success of your stand. Below is an example.

1   Number of visitor enquiries envisaged vs number of visitor enquiries taken.
2   Cost per sales lead v cost per field sales call.
3   Value of anticipated orders taken vs value of actual orders taken.
4   Evaluation of your stand's sales success in comparison to your competitors. (Were you up on the number of enquiries and sales conversions?)
5   Estimated number of visitor walk-ons compared to total show attendance.
6   Evaluation of your stand sales staff performance.

Sales achievements value

Sales and promotional analysis

Sales	Objectives	Result	Value £
New client enquiries	10	8	10,000
Sales to new clients	2	3	4,000
Sales to existing clients	4	6	8,000
New product – new clients	3	6	6,000
New product – established existing clients	4	5	5,000

Marketing and Promotions

Number of new enquiries	20		
Existing client enquiries	12		

	Objectives	Result	Value £
Marketing and Promotions			
New product enquiries	12		
Press attendance at product launch,			
target 40, actual 45	5	7	
volume of literature			
handed out	10,000	8,000	
Press visits	8	8	

Sales follow-up

Sales leads obtained from exhibitions are invaluable and a special plan of action should be devised to turn these leads into actual sales. For most exhibitors, if they achieve better than average sales as previously targeted then the event will be seen as a success. Enquiry leads take two forms: (1) stand visitor sales enquires from walking around the show; (2) promotional-based leads (as a result of an advertisement or promotional attraction).

The time scale involved in following up these leads depends on the volume of orders taken during the show, the existing service to clients, in short the number of available man-hours. However, whatever happens, these leads must not be allowed to go 'cold'. Appointments should be made as soon after the exhibition as possible; any additional information should, as a priority, be mailed out or delivered.

The conversion rate of these sales leads depends on the professionalism of your sales team and on the value of the enquiry in the first instance. A nil result should not always be blamed on the latter.

You will no doubt receive enquiries from existing customers and these should be passed on to the sales representative who deals with that customer on an ongoing basis. It is important when this does occur to ensure that this order is seen as one obtained from the exhibition and not one received in the normal course of events.

Ask your sales manager to compile on a weekly basis any sales achieved as a direct result of sales leads deriving from the exhibition, stating the value and size of the order. You will need to compile all this information (internal and external sources) before coming to a decision on whether or not the exhibition was a success.

Checklist – promotional achievements

1 Has the targeted audience been reached?
2 Did the organisers' promotional activities match up to expectations, and did they assist in the company's own promotional activities?
3 Was the stand more successful than its competitors in attracting visitors?
4 Did the exhibition as a promotional tool mix well with the company's overall sales and marketing plan?
5 Did pre-exhibition publicity achieve its intended objectives?
6 Has post-exhibition publicity achieved its intended objectives?
7 What was the reaction of both visitors and staff to:
   • Location and site;
   • Size and design of stand;
   • Hospitality arrangements;

- Demonstrations;
- Publicity gained;
- Literature;
- Stand management;
- Sales information and follow-up.

8 How much would it have cost to achieve the same promotional success without using the exhibition as a vehicle?
9 Was the exhibition a success from the number of actual sales and potential sales?
10 How acute was the organisers' targeting of visitors?
11 Has there been any new reaction towards your products?
12 Has any new product knowledge presented itself?
13 Does the event compare favourably with the last one? Detail reasons for and against.
14 Was the event within the promotional budget?

Interpreting organisers' statistics

Statistics given out by the organisers after the event should primarily be looked at for the type of visitor to the show. The number of visitors to the show is secondary if your aim was an increase in the number of sales conversions.

Identify whether the attendance was up in relation to the target in:

- Total number of attendance;
- Status;
- Decision-making (therefore purchasing power);
- Industry category;
- Other.

In other words, was the quality and quantity of visitors up to the targeted requirements?

Evaluating costs

You or your stand manager should have signed for any item ordered during the exhibition, including small-cost items such as additional drinks for hospitality. Prior to the opening of the exhibition certain invoices will have had to be settled.

Ask your accounts office to photocopy each invoice relating to the exhibition and send you a copy.

With your budget sheet compare estimated costs with actual costs. Where these costs differ, insert an explanation – not all costs will be more than those estimated, you might have overpriced a particular item of expenditure.

To work out indirect costs such as the time your staff took to prepare the exhibit and to man the stand, create the number of hours into working days (provided of course you do not pay additional rates for overtime, in which case you will have to add this cost on separately). This then becomes a simple mathematical exercise.

Assessing what sales were achieved is more difficult. What criteria, for example, will you set on sales achieved? Suppose Widget & Co. were going to buy your latest machines but the order was secured at the exhibition. Would you include this as revenue achieved from the exhibition? Or would you say that it was revenue achieved from the normal course of business? Suppose an order has not yet been signed up. Would you include the value of this in the revenue? Most certainly not, but your calculation will be over when the order is realised.

Once you have identified the sales revenue criteria then ask the sales manager for a list of orders so that the accounts department can trace the invoiced amount and present you with the exact figure. Again, you can compare the estimated figure with the actual.

To quantify the value of PR gained from exhibiting is extremely difficult, if not impossible. Did you really need the extra exposure? How much would you have paid for it? Were any sales made as a result of it?

When evaluating the success of the stand do not let its success or failure ride solely on the amount expended. Naturally, you do not want to be wasteful with your company's resources but the reality of success or failure is not so 'cut and dried' as accountants like to make it.

A good exhibition will be apparent by the climate it stimulates; both visitors and fellow exhibitors are likely to tell you what they think of the event. In particular, the mood of the exhibitors on the final day is usually a good indicator of how good, bad or indifferent the exhibition has been. Take a walk around the event for a few minutes on the final afternoon and ask a few pertinent questions; while this will not give you a statistical evaluation it will give you a good idea of the quality of an event.

Checklist – expenditure v revenue

Item	Estimated cost £	Actual cost £
Space rental		
Design and construction		
Pre-publicity:		
direct		
indirect		
Printed material		
Display material		
Entertainment		
Accommodation		
Exhibits		
Staff costs:		
direct		
indirect		
Cost per sales enquiry		
Revenue achieved		
Immediate sales		
Short-term conversionary sales		
Medium/long-term orders:		
anticipated		
received		
	———	———
Total		

The final evaluation

Each of you will have different objectives and therefore only you can evaluate whether or not the event has been of benefit to you. This section serves to reiterate and remind you of your objectives before you cast your judgement.

Often, advantages cannot be specifically quantified without drawing upon the experiences of previous events or attempting to judge how well your company's stand, its sales generation, publicity and so on fared against your competitors.

Consult your list of main objectives and see whether your analysis of the different areas fulfils their requirements. Here, if you have placed an unrealistic target on, say, sales, then it is unlikely that this objective will have been met. Likewise, if your accounts show that expenditure has been overshot by a couple of hundred pounds then this does not mean that the show has been a failure. Create a scale of 1 to 10 and determine what level on the scale was achieved by each component.

With the evaluation of your objectives, put together a full and detailed report. You will need this internal survey of the event when deciding on future policy.

At the end, with the exhibition behind you, with all this collated information to hand and your evaluation report on the table, remember to keep the data in a safe place for future reference. The information gives a clear view of what can be done to turn the bad points around so that benefits can be gained when participating in future events.

9

Exhibiting overseas

Since 1977 the amount of money spent by British companies exhibiting overseas has risen threefold per annum. These exhibitors have been greatly helped in achieving maximum success by the Department of Trade and Industry (DTI), which helps to promote British goods and services overseas.

When first considering participating in an overseas event, remember that the lead time necessary to prepare for the exhibition has got to be extended. More time is needed in researching market suitability and so on. Other areas which also need attention will be accommodation, transportation, the number of translations needed for all your exhibition leaflets etc. Help on these matters can be obtained from many sources, from the International Chamber of Commerce to the Central Office of Information. Addresses for these organisations are in the Appendix.

The Department of Trade and Industry

The Fairs and Promotions Branch (FPB) of the DTI provides financial and other assistance to British companies wishing to participate on a group basis, in selected overseas trade fairs. The scheme of support is operated in conjunction with a number of approved sponsoring trade associations or Chambers of Commerce, and applies to some 300 overseas trade fairs each year. The list of events at which assistance under the scheme is available is published as a quarterly supplement in the Department's journal, *British Business*. Information is also available from the DTI Regional Offices and from Fairs and Promotions Branch itself.

Under the terms of the DTI scheme, the sponsoring body recruits a group of British companies (usually a minimum of 10) which wish to exhibit British goods and/or services at one of the selected overseas trade fairs. The DTI provides stands and display aids for the group at subsidised rates; the level of subsidy for each company in the group depends upon the number of times it has participated at the trade fair in the past. Apart from the obvious financial attractions, the DTI scheme also offers the considerable advantage of removing much of the organisational chores from the participating firms by arranging for the construction of exhibition stands. This makes it particularly attractive to companies that are new to exhibiting overseas, especially small and medium-sized companies.

Generally, small and medium-sized companies who have not exhibited overseas before tend to have the opinion that exhibiting is not cost effective and takes up too much of their company's man-hours. This is certainly not the case. As far as costs for overseas events are concerned, in Germany for instance, an exhibitor from the UK would find that having an exhibition stand at one of that country's events could cost less than if he were to exhibit at one of the UK events and with DTI support could be extremely cost effective. Indirect costs such as accommodation, entertaining etc, can vary considerably from country to country. Check out the cost before booking. Ask your travel agent what the cost of living is like compared with the UK to get an idea of what to expect.

If considering exhibiting at an overseas exhibition that does not have a UK group stand, talk to the Central Office of Information and also the embassies of the countries that you intend to exhibit in. Gain as much information as you can from them, learn the intricacies of their own individual selling culture. Make yourself familiar with people's likes and dislikes, how they react to sales, and so on.

The terminology surrounding overseas sites also differs. In America you hire a booth rather than a stand. In the US, companies tend not to go for large specifically designed stands in the way that their counterparts do in the UK. Instead, you might take two or maybe three booths, all open, with shelving for a display of posters and carousel units for leaflets. Large mobile displays are usually not part of the exhibition scene in the US.

Cultural communications

Different styles of operation influence your exhibition stand when participating in an overseas event. You will no doubt meet people from many different countries. You have to relate in different ways to different cultures. Even the most common areas can change. For example, not only do visual meanings differ but the spoken word too – despite the same language – can be interpreted differently. English, the most widely used of languages, can cause disastrous results when for example a foreign visitor who has a seemingly perfect command of that language misunderstands one word or phrase.

Colour and design also play a part when presenting your product abroad. Our European partners for example have a different perspective when relating to colour. The Germans prefer bold, vivid colours which would be offputting to the French who prefer more pastel shades. This is where a discussion with the organisers is essential; they should be able to give you all the information needed on how to go about

manning and designing your stand and the different selling approaches with your stand visitors. Remember, organisers are approachable people and you are paying them money to participate in their event so they should give you their full attention. The Central Office of Information specialises in supplying information on a wide spectrum of topics on countries overseas. It is wise to talk to the COI as the wealth of information that is available (from attitudes to expectations) is difficult to find anywhere else.

Shipping procedures

If attending an event organised by the DTI or by one of their authorised organisers, then the shipping procedures are simplified. The DTI or their organisers give details of a UK site where delivery of all stand display material is to be delivered. This is then packaged and placed in a container along with cases from other members of the exhibiting group. The container is then shipped across to the venue site.

You will obviously need a longer lead time to collect and package all items before delivering them – and the relevant documentation supplied by the organiser – to the collection point. On page 98 you will find a description of procedures taken from the exhibitors' manual of the International Watch, Jewellery and Silver Trades Fair. Whilst the wording of the information will differ from organiser to organiser the details will basically be the same.

As you can see from the extract overleaf, the organisers will give you a date when the package will be available for reassembly at the overseas site. If you send your exhibits via the organisers then usually they will hire the electrical contractors on your behalf as part of the arrangements. On some sites you will be able to book your own authorised electrician or authorised stand contractor but you have to abide by the organisers' rules on this subject. Costs, however, are likely to be cheaper on a group scale via the organisers than if you are doing it on a one-off basis. If you do hire your own stand contractor then make sure he is aware of the build-up and breakdown schedules.

Whether you use the organisers' transportation services or not, adequate packaging of exhibits must be done. The cases used to transport the displays must be of sufficient strength

Transportation of exhibits

1.1 Recommended Shipping and Transportation Contractor

The Organisers have appointed the following company as the official transportation contractor for the exhibition:

I.E.S. Ltd,
Unit 1, Fairview Trading Estate,
Acton Lane,
London NW10 7NG
Tel: 01–965 9966   Telex: 915066   Fax: 01–965 1160

They will inform all exhibitors of the requirements of the local authorities and the documentation required for the entry of exhibits.

Exhibitors are strongly advised, in their own interests, and that of the exhibition as a whole, to use the services of this company which has experience in handling exhibition shipments and will supply comprehensive pre-exhibition, site and post-exhibition services. They will provide details of all documentation requirements and have the responsibility of supervising all movements within Dubai, with their on-site personnel co-ordinating the final installation.

All exhibitors will be advised by IES Ltd of the name and address of the sub-contractor appointed in their country.

IES Ltd will request from each exhibitor full details of exhibits in order that an overall installation programme may be formulated. [This date] may vary according to country of origin and the sub-contractor will advise accordingly.

The official contractors have total responsibility for the movement of all exhibits on the exhibition site and no other transportation control or their equipment will be allowed to enter the exhibition area without the written approval of the Organisers.

All packing materials, crates and cases will be stored off site following unpacking procedures by the official contractor and returned to the stands at the close of the exhibition ready for repacking and onward transmission.

---

to withstand handling methods. Cases should be constructed with sturdy bases, capable of withstanding movements via rollers, loading off trolleys and protecting the cargo inside. It is better if cases have prefabricated sections and can be bolted. They should be strong enough for use once the exhibition is over and repacking starts.

If independently exhibiting at an overseas event, the organisers of that event may have a group transportation scheme whereby your stand material can be brought across with other UK exhibitors, similar to package schemes previously mentioned. Do talk to the organisers to find out if this scheme does exist. If it does not and you are happy to organise the shipping procedures yourself, check with the COI and the relevant embassy whether there are any items of equipment to which import restrictions apply.

Another area to check up on is electricity voltage. You could find that any electrically operated carousels might not work because of the difference in voltage from country to country, so adaptors or rewiring might be necessary.

Pre-selling of some exhibits might have been arranged beforehand. If this is the case and a contract has been concluded prior to the start of the exhibition and shipment of the exhibit, you will have to apply for and obtain an import licence or permit.

Of course, you will have to obtain adequate insurance cover for damage to goods or loss of equipment while being shipped. This is in addition to the normal insurance cover which the organisers insist you obtain, as part of the booking procedure.

Whether you use the organisers' transportation or not you will have certain bills to meet – other than the hire of stand, etc. For example, you will have to pre-pay for customs clearance, which based on the value of the goods can amount to circa 4 per cent or so. This does differ from country to country. Failure to pay this obviously means that your exhibits will not clear customs.

Contact HM Customs and Excise and tell them what equipment you are taking overseas so that you can obtain an exemption form to bring the exhibits/displays back into this country. If this is not obtained then the goods could be judged by Customs and Excise as being purchased overseas and therefore subject to VAT. For each major item of equipment taken overseas an exemption form must be obtained.

Members of the EEC can reclaim expendables in fellow community-member countries, so all receipts and vouchers or original invoices should be held and attached to VAT Form 65. This form is obtainable from HM Customs and Excise. However, it must be submitted no later than one year after the event. A special form for application is available from the tax authority of the EEC country you are visiting. For ease of shipping, an ATA carnet document can be obtained from Chambers of Commerce. This document allows for temporary admission to any country which is party to the customs convention drawn up in 1961.

Whatever is itemised on the ATA carnet document must be returned to the country of origin; any items that are unlikely to be returned through breakages or disposables must be noted on a separate document. Mistakes made in this way can delay returning consignments through customs and could cause additional costs.

When transporting your exhibition items overseas, especially if using road haulage, make sure you are aware of any national holiday in the designated country or indeed through any country which the goods have to pass. This is relevant should you be shipping or containerising your exhibition goods.

One of the cheapest ways of getting your exhibit overseas is by container and then using sea links. Air links are rather expensive but of course the benefit is speed.

Exhibiting overseas need not be a tedious or time consuming job, rather it can initiate a great deal of contacts and overseas sales. But considerable ground work is needed beforehand. The same principles that are used when deciding whether to attend a particular venue, budgeting for the event, manning of the stand and so on apply as they would to a UK site but with different elements brought in. However, with proper planning the event can be highly successful and above all profitable for your business.

10

Taking stock – trade shows and consumer exhibitions

The difference between a consumer exhibition and a trade show is that the latter is primarily product and service orientated whilst the former is involved in direct selling to the public. As such, the stand, and what goes on, will differ as much as its atmosphere. This chapter is all about the difference and how to utilise either consumer or trade fairs in your exhibition programme.

Promotional link-ins

The organiser of a consumer show has to have a keen and alert imagination ready to react to any situation that can be used to the exhibition's advantage. Most trade shows have national coverage or coverage particular to the industry to which they relate. Whilst this may appear a lower key approach it is still no less valid. But with consumer shows the organiser usually relies heavily on the gate so it is in his best interests to gain as many visitors and therefore the maximum amount of publicity.

For the organiser, achieving the exact amount of 'spend' is the key to success. 'Spend' is the combination of direct 'spend': costs involved in gaining coverage on TV, radio, national and provincial advertisements, posters, car stickers and other items, coupled with indirect 'spend' such as PR to stimulate press feature articles etc.

A consumer exhibition today is preoccupied with selling; moving products directly off the stand or taking orders and deposits for immediate delivery. Direct selling opportunities are many and varied. Exhibitions attract people who wish to visit the show, giving you an attentive audience keen to see whatever there is on display. The items sold from consumer-orientated stands vary from a complete home at the Ideal Home Exhibition to more general, smaller items such as paintings at a craft fair.

Organisers themselves are keenly aware of the difference between a consumer and trade show as they often organise both types of events. Once the stands have been sold and the exhibition organised the key role of the organising companies is to generate as much publicity as possible to keep the interest alive. And this is where, if handled properly, the main benefit to stand holders occurs. Provided on-going liaison with the organiser's promotional department has been maintained, then linking into a publicity programme is possible. For example, the organiser might have laid on special events or press preview days or be working on a particular theme. This might have a direct influence on the sale of your products.

New events

When deciding on an exhibition programme, list all trade and consumer events that are directly linked to your products or your company's market anticipations. From time to time there will be new shows appearing. If interested in exhibiting at one of these you should ask the organiser the following questions to ascertain the value of the show to your needs.

1 Is he a member of the Association of Exhibition Organisers? Many reputable organisers are not. Be that little bit more wary with non-members as there are some less professional ones around too.
2 What is the organiser going to do regarding PR/promotions?
3 What other event/s have been organised? Ask to see the literature and the attendance figures;
4 Ask the organiser what other companies are taking stands at the exhibition. If you find that none of the market leaders is taking a stand try to find out why.

The benefit of attending a new consumer show is that the attendance figures are likely to be higher than those for other annual consumer shows because the promotion ratio on 'spend' for new shows usually increases in order to draw in the 'necessary gate', i.e. the number of visitors.

Remember, do not sign your contract until you are happy with the standard of the event, i.e. number of potential visitors, PR/promotions, number and type of exhibitors and so on. By all means reserve the stand space, but do not complete and send in your contract as once this is done payment becomes due. There is little or no recourse once the contract has been signed should the event not take off as anticipated.

Press participation

Trade shows attract the technical journals which report back to the industry involved. This is the primary source of publicity

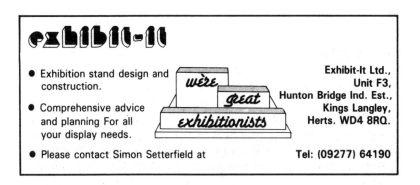

for these events. The secondary source is the provincial press who are also likely to attend. National press will only attend if the event is of interest. For consumer shows the order of press interest reverses itself.

The organiser will have previously sent out invitations along with press releases inviting the press to either a press day, press launch or similar event. You may also be invited to attend these events and it should be one of your major concerns to gain as much promotional coverage as possible.

Events are now often sponsored or co-sponsored by a magazine, journal or newspaper, in which case the editor will make a particular feature of the exhibition. Liaison with the organiser will enable you to gain as much publicity advantage as possible during any of these special events.

Follow the guidelines outlined on page 52 when writing press releases. Make sure that they have a specific interest or topic that will be of significant use to the paper or journal that they are sent to. Always keep in mind any item of news that can link in with the exhibition itself, such as an important person visiting your stand or the launch of a new product. Journalists are very busy people, and therefore they require items of interest, crisply presented and substantiated by facts. If you follow these rules then you will have a greater chance of press coverage.

Features

Ask the organiser (consumer or trade show) what features are planned. For trade shows ask the organiser if he is planning to have a technology or trade feature which would perhaps include all associations and related areas together in a particular part of the hall. If it is a consumer event, ask if there are any interesting features planned such as theatres, show houses and so on. Try to find out where these features will be placed in the exhibition hall. If your stand is close by, as the queues build up waiting to see what is in store you will have a static audience in front of your stand. If you are selling a machine for cutting potatoes into chips and there is a feature on fast foods, the ideal location would be opposite or alongside this feature as extra visitors to your stand are almost guaranteed.

However, the exhibition organiser does not often know

Top. *A themed stand at a communication show. The exhibitor designed the stand as an American ice cream parlour and employed lovely ladies on roller skates to serve ice cream to customers – a simple and effective stand.*

Bottom. *Many exhibitors benefited from a pancake world record competition organised by the exhibition press office. Everyone who supplied ingredients and equipment was featured as a sponsor. Always try to get involved in happenings at an exhibition – good exposure is usually the result.*

what features are planned as the ideas and opportunities for them arise once the exhibition has been launched. You should normally be able to see a plan of events which detail the features some three or four months beforehand. Should you find that you have booked a stand some distance away from a feature which is closely related to your product, you can ask the organiser to move your stand closer to it. The first exhibitors' list for a consumer show will be regularly updated and it is worth asking for new details every three to four weeks. For trade shows features are known well beforehand so that you can plan where your location should be.

Some exhibition organisers, especially for large consumer events, place exhibitors with similar products or in similar consumer fields together. You could find some 10 to 20 small stands in a particular area of the hall, covering both sides of the aisle. These avenues of trade are similar in marketing principle to the old-fashioned market stalls, they attract many people to one stand who then wander around the other stands.

Other than the points mentioned above, positioning is not now a main criterion when booking stand space, but avoid corners or backwaters. Previously, with consumer and trade fairs there used to be a rush to book stand space directly opposite the entrance. For years businesses used to jockey for this position. However, they have now found that visitors tend to walk straight into the show, often ignoring this stand. But on the way out, especially with children in tow, a stand selling small items of interest, e.g. computer games, will increase its sales. Visitors usually turn to the left when walking into the hall and leave via the right hand side. So the psychology of stand location, whilst less important, is still with us.

Selling from the stand – stand attractions

With the key point at a consumer show being direct selling, showing your product to its best advantage is important. If your product allows you to demonstrate or give your visitors a hands-on experience this will aid your sales. If your product does not allow you to do this then it is worth buying in animation of some sort to attract visitors to your stand. This applies to either trade or consumer shows.

The Manchester Exhibition and Events Centre, a medium-sized venue with some 10,300 square metres of space, converted from the Central Station terminal into an exhibition centre at the cost of £20 million.

The more people you attract to your stand the more product you are likely to sell. Demonstrations always attract people and the more interesting the demonstration the more people you attract. However, do not let it run on for too long; crowds are all very well but you want to sell your product and move on to the next batch of customers.

Always ensure that your gangway is not too small or liable to become blocked. Potential customers can be put off if access is difficult. If you expect large crowds then allow for a large free area in front of your stand.

Which type of event is best for you?

Few companies attend both consumer and trade exhibitions although some do – e.g., the Motor Show, when manufacturers, dealers and retailers are all present. The reason that companies select either trade or consumer events is because if their products are sold direct to the public then distribution outlets will be reluctant to get involved because of the

Top.   *Earls Court Exhibition Centre, London, during the British International Toy and Hobby Fair, 1989.*

Bottom.   *Olympia's Grand Hall with special ceiling treatment for Hotelympia, the International Hotel and Catering Exhibition.*

small profit margin. Neither would distribution outlets be pleased if they found that you were selling direct to the public. However, for major consumer events, this rule is often waived for exhibitions which attract both consumers and trade purchasers.

Selecting which exhibition is best for you is relatively a straightforward marketing choice. Do you currently rely on direct sales methods? Are you anticipating changing your sales approach? Do you use distributors or are you going to use distributors? Do you sell direct to the public in the UK and via distributors overseas? A combination might be better for you in this instance, i.e. via UK consumer shows and also via overseas trade events. As a rule of thumb, if you sell direct to the public then consumer fairs are normally selected and if selling into the trade then only trade exhibitions apply.

Conclusion

Exhibitions must be seen as part of your business's promotional programme, enabling you to meet the right people to sell your product or service in an atmosphere conducive to this objective. This is what exhibitions are all about.

However, an event itself does not mean that you will sell a greater supply of product than your salesforce on the road. It is how you turn that event to your advantage that makes it work for you. Nor do results from one event prove that exhibitions are good or bad for your business. It takes time for results from participation in different events to be analysed. Once this is done then judgement can be made.

How heavily you get involved in exhibiting and whatever your final decision is as to its success, there is no other promotional medium where your sales personnel can meet the right target audience in order to achieve potentially greater annual sales.

A successful professionally organised exhibition invariably creates a superb climate for business and is unrivalled in the area of direct sales and marketing.

The exhibition industry is currently experiencing a new renaissance in many parts of the world, but particularly in the United Kingdom. Effective use of exhibitions can maximise your company's sales potential and achieve additional benefits in the form of promotions, customer data and personal contact. Since the days of medieval markets and fairs, the exhibition medium has promoted the growth of trade; its modern equivalent is once again achieving unrivalled results as modern man goes to market to sell his wares, in order to gain that all-important competitive edge at a time when pressure to do so has never been greater.

While the modern equivalent of the market square has become a sophisticated forum with many facets, the modern day exhibition proves that personal contact is still the most beneficial way of doing business in today's hi-tech fast-moving business environment.

Appendix

Useful Addresses

Exhibition venues

Birmingham
National Exhibition Centre
Birmingham B40 1NT
021-780 4141

London
Earls Court Exhibition Centre
Warwick Road
London SW5 9TA
01-385 1200

Olympia
Hammersmith Road
London W14 8UX
01-603 3344

Kensington Exhibition Centre
99 Kensington High Street
London W8 5TD
01-937 9898

Wembley Conference Centre
Wembley HA9 0DW
01-902 8833

Alexandra Palace
Wood Green
London N22 4AY
01-883 6477

Barbican Exhibition Halls
Golden Lane
London EC2Y 8DS
01-588 8211

Business Design Centre
51 Upper Street
Islington
London N1 0QH
01-359 3535

London Arena
Lime Harbour
Isle of Dogs
London E14
01-538 8880

Novotel
1 Shortlands
Hammersmith
London W6 8DR
01-741 1555

Blackpool
Blackpool Winter Gardens
Church Street
Blackpool FY1 3PL
0253 25252

111

Brighton
Metropole Exhibition Hall
Kings Road
Brighton
Sussex BN1 2FU
0273 775432

Bristol
Bristol Exhibition Centre
2 Canon's Road
City Centre
Bristol BS1 5UH
0272 298630

Esher
Sandown Exhibition Centre
Esher
Surrey KT10 9AJ
0372 67540

Glasgow
Scottish Exhibition and
   Conference Centre
Glasgow G3 8YW
041-221 1769

Harrogate
Harrogate Exhibition Centre
Harrogate
North Yorkshire
0423 68051

Kenilworth
National Agricultural Centre
Stoneleigh
Warwickshire CV8 2LZ
0203 696969

Leicester
Leicester Exhibition Centre
Easham Boulevard
Leicester LE2 7BN
0533 548271

Manchester
G-Mex Centre
City Centre
Manchester M2 3BX
061-834 2700

Telford
Telford Exhibition Centre
St Quentin Gate
Telford
Shropshire TF3 4JH
0952 505522

Exhibition organisers

AGB Exhibitions Ltd
Audit House
Field End Road
Eastcote
Middlesex HA4 9XE
01-868 4499

Andry Montgomery Group
11 Manchester Square
London W1M 5AB
01-486 1951

Angex Ltd
Europa House
St Matthew Street
London SW1P 2JT
01-222 9341

Argus Press
Queensway House
2 Queensway
Redhill
Surrey RH1 1QS
0737 68611

Argus Specialist Exhibition Ltd
PO Box 35
Wolsey Road
Hemel Hempstead
Hertfordshire HP2 4SS
0442 41221

Batiste Exhibitions &
   Promotions
Pembroke House
Campsbourne Road
London N8 7PE
01-340 3291

Birmingham Post & Mail
   (Exhibition) Ltd
28 Colmore Circus
Birmingham B4 6AX
021-236 3366

Blenheim Exhibitions
   Group Plc
137 Blenheim Crescent
London W11 2EQ
01-727 1929

Blenheim Online Ltd
Blenheim House
Ash Hill Drive
Pinner
Middlesex HA5 2AE
01-868 4466

Blenheim PEL
   Communications
137 Blenheim Crescent
London W11 2EQ
01-727 1929

Brintex Ltd
178–202 Portland Street
London W1N 6NH
01-637 2400

Cahners Exhibitions Ltd
26 The Quadrant
Richmond
Surrey TW9 1DL
01-948 9900

Electrex Ltd
Wix Hill House
West Horsley
Surrey KT24 6DZ
0483 222888

EMAP Maclaren
   Exhibitions Ltd
840 Brighton Road
Purley
Surrey CR2 2BH
01-660 8008

Evan Steadman
   Communications Group
The Hub
Emson Close
Saffron Walden
Essex CB10 1HL
0799 26699

Focus Events Ltd
Greencoat House
Francis Street
London SW1P 1DG
01-834 1717

Independent Exhibitions Ltd
Waltrix House
Oak Road
Leatherhead
Surrey KT22 7PG
0372 372842

Industrial Newspapers Plc
2 Queensway
Redhill
Surrey RH1 1QS
0737 768611

Industrial Trade Fairs Ltd
Oriel House
The Quadrant
Richmond
Surrey TW9 1DL
01-948 9800/9900

Langfords Exhibitions Ltd
32 West Street
Brighton BN1 2RT
0273 206722

Mack-Brooks Exhibitions Ltd
Forum Place
Hatfield
Hertfordshire AL10 0RN
07072 75641

MGB Exhibitions Ltd
109 Station Road
Sidcup
Kent DA15 7ET
01-302 8585

Microwave Exhibitions &
   Publishers Ltd
90 Calverley Road
Tunbridge Wells
Kent TN1 2UN
0892 44027

Montbuild Ltd
11 Manchester Square
London W1M 5AB
01-486 1951

Naidex Conventions Ltd
90 Calverley Road
Tunbridge Wells
Kent TN1 2UN
0892 44027

National Boat Show Ltd
Boating Industry House
Vale Road
Oatlands
Weybridge
Surrey KT13 9NS
0932 854511

National Exhibition
   Centre Ltd
Exhibition Division
Birmingham B40 1NT
021-780 4171

Network Exhibitions &
   Conferences Ltd
Printers Mews
Market Hill
Buckingham MK18 1JK
0280 815226

Philbeach Events Ltd
Earls Court Exhibition Centre
Warwick Road
London SW5 9TA
01-385 1200

Pinnacle Events Ltd
Trinity House
Hercies Road
Hillingdon
Middlesex UB10 9NA
0895 72277

Plus Shows Ltd
23 Farmham Close
Bracknell
Berkshire RG12 3AX
0344 486385

Reed Exhibition
   Companies Ltd
Oriel House
26 The Quadrant
Richmond
Surrey TW9 1DL
01-948 9900

SEC Exhibitions Ltd
Scottish Exhibition and
   Conference Centre
Glasgow G3 8YW
041-221 1769

Smithfield Show Joint
   Committee
Forbes House
Halkin Street
London SW1X 7DS
01-235 0315

Swan House Special
   Events Ltd
Holly Road
Hampton Hill
Middlesex TW12 1PZ
01-783 0055

Trades Exhibitions Ltd
Exhibition House
Spring Street
London W2 3RB
01-262 2886

Trade Promotion Services Ltd
Exhibition House
Warren Lane
London SE18 6BW
01-855 9201

Trinity Group
Trinity House
Hercies Road
Hillingdon
Middlesex UB10 9NA
0895 58431

Trade associations

Exhibition Industry Federation
Sheen Lane House
254 Upper Richmond Road
   West
London SW14 8AG
01-878 9130

Association of Exhibition
   Organisers (AEO)
207 Market Towers
Nine Elms Lane
London SW8 5NQ
01-627 3946

British Exhibition Contractors
   Association
Kingsmere House
Graham Road
London SW19 3SR
01-543 3888

British Exhibition Venues
   Association
'Mallards'
Five Ashes
Mayfield
East Sussex TN20 6NN
0435 872244

National Association of
   Exhibition Hallowners
National Exhibition Centre
Birmingham B40 1NT
021-780 4141

Government assistance

Central Office of Information
Hercules House
Westminster Bridge Road
London SE1 7DU
01-928 2345

Department of Trade and
  Industry
1 Victoria Street
London SW1H 0ET
01-215 7877

Overseas fairs and outward missions

Fairs and Promotions Branch
Dean Bradley House
52 Horseferry Road
London SW1P 2AG
01-212 0093/6277

Exhibition services

Animated display

Absolute Action Ltd
Mantle House
Broomhill Road
London SW18 4JQ
01-871 5005

Applied Audio Visual Ltd
Capitol House
662 London Road
Cheam
Surrey SM3 9BY
01-644 6194

British Turntable Co Ltd
Emblem Works
Bolton
Lancashire
0204 25626

Technamation
Southdown Studios
Osiers Road
London SW18
01-874 4152

Artificial grass

Norman Witcomb Exhibition
  Services
Unit 27
Exhibition Way
National Exhibition Centre
Birmingham B40 1PJ
021-780 3826

Audio visual

HSS Sightsound
London
Unit 2
St Pancras Commercial Centre
63 Pratt Street
London NW1 0BY
01-482 5232

HSS Sightsound
Midlands
1026 Coventry Road
Birmingham B25 8DP
021-773 3350

Instead Hire Birmingham
1 Hylton Place
Hylton Street
Hockley
Birmingham B18 6HN
021-551 7871

London & East Anglia Video &
  AV Hire
A1 Park Lane Video
Robjohn's House
Navigation Road
Chelmsford
Essex CM2 6ND
0245 350537

Samuelson Communications
  Ltd (Birmingham)
372–376 Summer Lane
Newton
Birmingham B19 3QA
021-233 2999

Badges

CES Marketing Ltd
40 Moor Street
Coventry
Warwickshire CV5 6EQ
0203 715001

Markovits Istvan
1-3 Cobbold Mews
London W12 9LB
01-749 3000

Banner makers

Denigraphic Associates Ltd
381 Folkestone Road
Dover CT15 9JR
0304 214022

Impact Graphics & Display Ltd
The Old Forge
273 Sandycombe Road
Kew
Surrey TW9 3LU
01-940 7418

Target Signs & Graphics
1a Tennison Road
London SE25 5SA
01-771 6992

Barriers, ropes, etc.

Giltspur International Ltd
Unit 2 Central Park Estate
Staines Road
Hounslow
Middlesex TW4 5DT
01-572 2121

HSS Event Hire Service Ltd
Unit 5
National Exhibition Centre
Birmingham B40 1PJ
021-780 3022/3516

Marler Haley Exposystems Ltd
18-20 Sandy Lane
Aston
Birmingham B6 5TP
021-327 5564

Nimlok Ltd
19a Floral Street
London WC2E 9DS
01-379 7289

Card and leaflet holders

J Thomas Edwards
  & Sons Ltd
Unit 15
2nd Exhibition Avenue
National Exhibition Centre
Birmingham B40 1NT
021-780 2428

Carpets

Giltspur International Ltd
Unit 2 Central Park Estate
Staines Road
Hounslow
Middlesex TW4 5DT
01-572 2121

HSS Event Hire Service Ltd
Unit 5
National Exhibition Centre
Birmingham B40 1PJ
021-780 3022/3516

Reeds Carpeting Contractors
Unit 6
207 Torrington Avenue
Coventry CV4 9AP
0203 694114

Carrier bags

Keenpac Polythene
   Supplies Ltd
Sovereign House
Princess Road West
Leicester LE1 6TR
0533 470544

Celebrities

Celebrity Projects Stage &
   Television Artistes
   Representation Ltd
S/T/A/R House
39 Star Street
London W2 1QB
01-724 4343

Children's playcare centres

World of Children Ltd
10 Lincoln Park Business
   Centre
Cressex
High Wycombe
Buckinghamshire HP12 3RD
0494 25051

Demonstrators and stand staff

Claire Barker Associates Ltd
London Office
15 Brackenbury Gardens
London W6 0BP
01-740 8075

Judy Gould Enterprises
Green Cottage
Ilmington
Shipston-on-Stour
Warwickshire CV36 4LA
0608 882 477

Electrical contractors

Beck Electrical Services Ltd
67 Alderbrook Road
London SW12 8AD
01-673 2020

United Exhibition Services Ltd
Office & Work
Unit 13
Perimeter Road
National Exhibition Centre
Birmingham B40 1PJ
021-780 2610

Electronic signs

A Complete Moving Message
   Service
2a Felstead Road
London E11 2QJ
01-989 3125

Microsign Exhibition Rentals
69a Gowan Avenue
London SW6 6RH
01-736 6747

Exhibition consultants

Aardvark Designs Ltd
25 Darin Court
Crown Hill
Milton Keynes MK8 0AD
0908 560234

Communication by Design
6 The Courthouse
38 Kingsland Road
London E2 8DD
01-729 4000

Firebank Kempster Group
Holland House
6 Church Street
Old Isleworth
Middlesex TW7 6BG
01-847 5001

Lynx Exhibition Services Ltd
143c High Street
Brentwood
Essex CM14 4SA
0277 214587

Pullman Design Group
271 Boston Road
London W7 2AT
01-579 4499

Floral decorators

H Ashton & Sons
92 School Road
Hockley Heath
Solihull B94 6RB
056 43 2235

Giltspur International Ltd
Unit 2 Central Park Estate
Staines Road
Hounslow
Middlesex TW4 5DT
01-572 2121

HSS Event Hire Services Ltd
Unit 5
National Exhibition Centre
Birmingham B40 1PJ
021-780 3022/3516

Furniture

Camden Furniture Hire Ltd
9/11 Silver Road
White City Industrial Park
London W12 7RJ
01-749 1642

Giltspur International Ltd
National Exhibition Centre
Birmingham B40 1PJ
021-780 2011

HSS Event Hire Services Ltd
Unit 5
National Exhibition Centre
Birmingham B40 1PJ
021-780 3022/3516

Graphics

Aardvark Designs Ltd
25 Darin Court
Crown Hill
Milton Keynes MK8 0AD
0604 37293

Alpha Graphics
56-58 Dunster Street
Northampton NN1 3JY
0604 37293

Berkswell Graphics & Signs
The Old Forge
Balsal Street
Balsal Common
West Midlands CV7 7AP
0676 32011

Hedges Wright (Bristol) Ltd
Gatton Road
Bristol BS2 9TF
0272 541921

Photobition Ltd
Byam Street
London SW6 2RG
01-736 1331

Holography

Light Fantastic Plc
4e–f Gelders Hall Road
Shepshed
Leicestershire LE12 9NH
0509 600220

Hotel booking agencies

Expotel
Banda House
Cambridge Grove
Hammersmith
London W6 0LE
01-741 4468

Insurance

Conference & Exhibition
    Insurance Services
33 Harbour Exchange Square
London E14 9GG
01-538 9840

Landscape contractors

H Ashton & Sons
92 School Road
Hockley Heath
Solihull B94 6RB
056 43 2235

Giltspur International Ltd
Unit 2 Central Park Estate
Staines Road
Hounslow
Middlesex TW4 5DT
01-572 2121

Laser effects

Laser Creation Ltd
55 Merthyr Terrace
London SW13 9DL
01-741 5747

Lighting

Concord Fitting Hire
Unit 14 Fortune Way
Salter Street
London NW10 6UF
01-960 6111

Stage Two Hire Service
197 Watford Road
Croxley Green
Rickmansworth
Hertfordshire
0923 30789

Mobile exhibition trailers

AH-HA Southern Mobile
53 School Lane
Bushey
Hertfordshire WD2 1BY
01-950 5051

Exhibition Vehicle Services Ltd
70–72a The Centre
Feltham
Middlesex TW13 4BH
01-890 0650

Photographers

Alpha Photographic Services
Unit 13
Chelsea Fields
278 Western Road
London SW19 2QA
01-648 1444

Post Studios
22 Colmore Circus
Birmingham B4 6AX
021-236 3366

Ted Edwards Photography
267 Wyndhurst Road
Stechford
Birmingham B33 9SL
021-784 5675

Photographic enlargements

Clements Graphic Services Ltd
Hanbury Road
Stoke Prior
Bromsgrove
Worcestershire B90 4AA
0527 35777

Photobition Ltd
Byam Street
London SW6 2RG
01-736 1331

Replicards Ltd
Replica House
Bavaria Road
London N19 4EX
01-272 6241

Public address and radio

Carpenter Audio Visual Ltd
Skyport House
Bath Road
West Drayton
Middlesex
01-759 4711

HSS Sightsound
London
Unit 2
St Pancras Commercial Centre
63 Pratt Street
London NW1 0BY
01-482 5232

Onsite Communications Ltd
Eaton House
Great North Road
Eaton Socon
St Neots
Cambridgeshire PE19 3EG
0480 405540

Security

NEC Ltd
Birmingham B40 1NT
021-780 4141

Sterling Security Service
    (Exhibitions Division)
Olympia 2
Exhibition Centre
Hammersmith Road
London W14 8UX
01-371 1339

Sign writing

Joe Manby Ltd
51–53 East Parade
Harrogate HG1 5LQ
0423 506191

Perton Signs Ltd
39–41 Margravine Road
London W6 8LL
01-381 6118

Stand construction

Beck & Pollitzer Contracts Ltd
Carlton House
106–118 Garratt Lane
London SW18 4DJ
01-874 0499

Central Display
  Productions Ltd
Norwood Road
Bordsley Green
Birmingham B9 5HU
021-773 8441

Images International
Unit 10
Station Industrial Estate
Sheppard Street
Swindon
Wiltshire SN1 5DB
0793 641581

Silver Knight Exhibitions Ltd
Unit 27
Elmdon Trading Estate
Bickenhill Lane
Birmingham B37 7HF
021-779 5551

Stanco Display Ltd
Units 4b/6/7
Second Exhibition Avenue
National Exhibition Centre
Birmingham B40 1PJ
021-780 2514

Team Construction Ltd
Unit 1
Team Industrial Estate
Sunny Bank Road
Mirfield
Yorkshire WF14 0JR
0924 494395

United Exhibition Services Ltd
Brook House
229–43 Shepherds Bush Road
London W6 7AN
01-741 7361

Further Reading

Trade publications

British Business
The Department of Trade
  and Industry
Dean Bradley House
52 Horseferry Road
London SW1P 2AG

*Exhibition and Conference Fact
  Finder*
Pembroke House
Campsbourne Road
London N8 7PE
01-340 3291

Exhibition Bulletin
272 Kirkdale
London SE26 4RZ
01-778 2288

Exhibitions and Conferences
70 Abingdon Road
London W8 6AP
01-937 6636

The Exhibitor
Media House
The Square
Forest Row
Sussex RH18 5EP
0342 824044

Business books

Telegraph publications

Britain on Business
How to Export
How to Set Up and Run Conferences and Meetings
How to Set Up and Run Your Own Business
Making Your Business Efficient
Marketing Your Business

Kogan Page

Be Your Own PR Man: Practical Public Relations for the Small Business, Michael Bland, 2nd edn 1987
Customer Service: How to Achieve Total Customer Satisfaction, Malcolm Peel, 1987
Do Your Own Market Research, Paul N Hague and Peter Jackson, 1987
Getting Sales: A Practical Guide to Getting More Sales for Your Business, R D Smith and G Dick, 1984
Effective Advertising for the Small Business, H C Carter, 1986
A Handbook of Advertising Techniques, Tony Harrison, 1987
How to Advertise, Kenneth Roman and Jane Maas, 1979
How to Promote Your Own Business: A Guide to Low Budget Publicity, Jim Dudley, 1987
The Industrial Market Research Handbook, Paul N Hague, 2nd edn 1987
Practical Sponsorship, Stuart Turner, 1987
Promoting Yourself on Television and Radio, Michael Bland and Simone Mondesir, 1987
Successful Marketing for the Small Business, Dave Patten, 2nd edn 1989

Index